The King's Grocer
The Life of Sir Thomas Lipton
by
Bob Crampsey

The King's Grocer

The Life of Sir Thomas Lipton

by

Bob Crampsey

GLASGOW CITY LIBRARIES

Crampsey, Bob
The King's Grocer. The Life of Sir Thomas Lipton.
ISBN 0-906169-43-7 (paperback)
ISBN 0-906169-44-5

© Glasgow City Libraries 1995
Published by Glasgow City Libraries Publications Board
The Mitchell Library, North Street, Glasgow, G3 7DN.

All photographs in this book are from the Sir Thomas Lipton
Collection, The Mitchell Library, except those supplied by
Unilever Archives, acknowledged individually.
This publication has been supported by Lipton Limited.

CONTENTS

Acknowledgements

This book has been written to accompany a major exhibition covering the life and work of Sir Thomas Lipton held at Glasgow Royal Concert Hall in the last quarter of 1995.

The exhibition marks the culmination of three years work to restore, preserve and catalogue the collection of photographs, press cuttings and other material which was bequeathed to the Mitchell Library in Glasgow on Thomas Lipton's death.

The library wishes to thank the Lipton Companies and Unilever which have both funded and supported the restoration work, the exhibition and this publication.

Special thanks are due to John Wotherspoon of Lipton Limited, whose personal enthusiasm and commitment have been inspirational.

Thanks also to Jeanette Strickland of Unilever Archives for permission to use some of their wonderful illustrations and to the members of Glasgow City Libraries Publications Board, especially Karen Cunningham, curator of the Lipton Collection at the Mitchell Library for additional research, selection of illustrations and editorial work; Elizabeth Carmichael; Verina Litster, graphic designer; and Moira Thorburn, photographer.

1995

The *Glasgow Herald* of 10th May, 1850 faithfully discharged its self-proclaimed role as "the world's intelligencer". Its reporting was anything but parochial and those who took the trouble to read it on that day would be tolerably well-informed about global affairs.

The steamship *Hermann* had arrived at Southampton with news from the United States which the paper cautiously validated only up to the 20th April. The news was that there was no news since "the great slavery question has for the nonce been postponed". Under the column headed Latest News one could learn of the increasing discontent with the Second Republic in France before somewhat disconcertingly picking up on the line below some fancied tips for the Chester Spring Meeting. On the lower Danube swarms of locusts were playing havoc with young crops.

In the shipping list Glasgow vessels were reported at Trinidad, Barbados, Panama and Quebec. Much of the population of Scotland was on the move westwards and a whole column was devoted to the attractions of the various emigrant ships. The sailing ship *Wandsworth*, master George Dunlop, was "Particularly airy and well-lit with nine feet headroom between decks". In conveying emigrants to Canada it would provision them amply. Each passenger would receive 8 pounds of bread in addition to biscuits, flour, oatmeal or rice, sugar and molasses while a liberal tea allowance was also supplied. The frigate *Speed* slightly trumped this offer with the proud statement that she would carry a surgeon on board. Sir John Ross was recruiting sailors on the West coast of Scotland for an Arctic voyage to cast light on the disappearance of Sir John Franklin's earlier expedition.

For those intending to emigrate from a stronger financial base there were sugar estates to be purchased in Trinidad or farmland for the asking in Cape Province. Clearly this was the newspaper of a city with broad and confident horizons.

Nearer home virtue and vice contended as they had done from the dawn of time. The trustees of the Normal School or Normal Seminary as it was then called had recently performed their annual visit of inspection and pronounced themselves much satisfied with the standard of learning achieved and the evidence of piety displayed. As the trustees were overwhelmingly ministers of the Church of Scotland this latter testimony could reasonably be supposed to carry weight.

Rewarding was the tale of the young boy who having found a purse of gold containing £20, took steps to return it to the police. The loser, a lady bound for Dublin was sufficiently grateful to give the lad £2 to which the magistrate added another. From the bench he contrasted the splendid action of the boy with that of two reprobates who having found £40 in the Cattle Market had spent half of it in dissipation and folly and when apprehended were well on the way to make inroads on the remainder. They received 60 days, the honest youth £3 and the magistrate's observation that "a wise son makes a glad father".

An unfortunate young woman threw herself into the river but cries were heard by a passing sailor. Dragged from the Clyde the girl proved to be the madam of the most notorious brothel in Glasgow. The madam, Ann Meek, was in an advanced state of intoxication when brought before the magistrate, Bailie Pearson. He reprimanded the prisoner severely because of the notoriety she had gained in Glasgow. He expressed the hope that she would seriously reflect on the evils of her past life and the rash attempt she had just made to deprive herself of existence. He ended by admonishing her to conduct herself with more propriety in the future and since she appeared unable to find the two guineas which she had been fined he made order that she should therefore serve the 60 days in prison which was the alternative.

The nineteenth century was at its midpoint. The Poet Laureate William Wordsworth who so embodied the early part of it had just been buried. There was a change from the pastoral to the urban industrial. The Scottish colliers were on strike and although the *Glasgow Herald* conceded that their request to be paid weekly rather than monthly was eminently reasonable, it was worried by the appearance in Scotland of "spouters", officials from mining areas in the North of England.

The great staple of newspapers was there in the Intimations section with seemingly every other death that of an infant child. There was but a handful of births recorded and that of the boy who was by far the most notable Glaswegian delivered that day was not among them. The *Glasgow Herald* cost the daunting sum of 4d and Mr. and Mrs. Thomas Lipton could not afford to buy it, far less place a birth notice in it. The entry into the world of Thomas Johnstone Lipton therefore was comparatively unregarded. His leavetaking would be a very different matter.

The life of Sir Thomas Johnstone Lipton presents certain difficulties for anyone attempting a biography. The major impediment can be described thus, that for the first twenty-five years of his life we know almost nothing of him, save what he himself cares to tell us, while for the remaining fifty-five years we know almost everything.

This is a double pity in that his boyhood and young manhood were of themselves fascinating and unusual but Lipton himself was the only recollector of them - he does not seem to have committed anything to paper as a young man - and he did not unburden himself to his first biographer William Blackwood until the last year of his life. By then there was no companion of his early years to act as reviser and if need be offer correction, assuming that Sir Thomas would have accepted it. Inevitably, therefore, the old man's recollection was from time to time imperfect and because of this, plus a not unnatural desire to shade certain events in his youth in his favour, the book, *Leaves from the Lipton Logs*, ostensibly an autobiography but clearly largely the work of Blackwood, raises certain assumptions that need to be examined.

Thomas Johnstone Lipton was born on May 10th 1850 at 10 Crown Street in the Hutchesontown district of Glasgow. The tenement flat had four rooms, one of which was occupied semi-permanently by lodgers, and was far from being a hovel. Indeed it belonged to the class of house so typical of Glasgow at that time, "respectable working class", for Lipton's life story does not fall into the category of Log Cabin to White House so beloved in his second country, the United States.

By one of those historical twists which make the subject so fascinating, another boy had been born a few hundred yards away some twenty years before who was to exercise a profound influence on that very White House. He was Allan Pinkerton who after serving his apprenticeship as a cooper and undergoing a youthful flirtation with Chartism, emigrated to the United States. There he formed the highly-successful and world famous Pinkerton Detective Agency.

Arguably, the younger of the two Scots, Thomas Johnstone Lipton would exercise even more influence on and in the United States. He was the last of five children of whom two were already dead at the time of his birth. Neither of the other two, his brother John or his sister Margaret, gave any great promise of longevity and in fact both died young. Given that Mrs. Lipton was in her early forties when she learned that she was expecting another child, it was an anxious pregnancy at a time when infant mortality was high.

The youngest child had from the start the vitality that his elder siblings so grievously lacked. It was as if he had drawn vitality

Thomas Lipton at the age of 12

Lipton's father

from the burgeoning city itself for he had arrived on the scene at a time of unparalleled civic and regional expansion.

By 1850 Glasgow was fast becoming a teeming city, quite altered in character from the little university town that had been so lavishly praised by Daniel Defoe at the beginning of the eighteenth century. It had lost its exclusively Lowland Scottish character and the two strains of the Gael, Highland and Irish had begun to predominate. Driven from the north of Scotland by the Highland Clearances and, often, ambition, harried across the Irish Sea by famine, the incomers were packed into insanitary warrens of tenements thrown up to house the vast labour force for which the iron masters and colliery owners of the West of Scotland were crying out. Further, to create an irresistible commercial and industrial impetus, Glasgow was better placed than any other British port to take advantage of the burgeoning trade with the fast-growing young Republic across the Atlantic.

The parents of Thomas Lipton had crossed from Ireland some years before. They were Ulster folk and their native country was the small village of Shannock Mills near the market town of Clones in County Monaghan and here we run up against the first of the assertions in *Leaves from the Lipton Logs* which perhaps should not go unchallenged.

In conversations in later years Lipton would leave the impression that his parents had been driven from Ireland by the Great Famine of 1845-48 but this seems unlikely for a variety of reasons. It is true that no county in Ireland emerged completely unscathed from the Great Hunger but the effect of it was markedly less felt in Ulster than in the western counties. A cruel paradox existed in the fact that the other crops flourished while the potatoes failed and in the county of Monaghan there was none of the almost total reliance on the coarse lumper potato which proved so disastrous in the far west. Again, Clones was on the border of Fermanagh, good Unionist country and distress there on the scale that Sligo and Clare were suffering would have been tackled with considerable vigour by the British Government.

This is not to say that the Liptons would have had an easy time of it in the hamlet of Shannock Mills. Monaghan was not exempt from the great weakness of Irish agriculture, the sub-division of land holdings that were already too small to be viable. It seems likely, however, that the motivating force behind the elder Lipton's decision to cross the Irish Sea was simply the realisation that Scotland offered much more in the way of opportunity for a man who wished to make his way, however modestly.

He was a good proposition for any employer for he was sober and industrious, presenting those virtues which mid-Victorians so prized, and he soon found employment in a warehouse which made cardboard boxes before moving up to become a time-keeper in a papermill in McNeill Street.

It is an oddity in the junior Lipton's recollections that he never mentions his mother by her christian name. She was nevertheless the influence that, from the outset, shaped his life. As with many families his mother was the lynchpin, the capable manager who yet had a touch of imagination and vision for her youngest son. In his earliest years Lipton was much around the house, being much too young to be a credible companion for his elder brother John. He seems to have talked much to his mother and listened as tales and songs of Ireland tumbled from her lips.

This leads us to another mystery which it will be as well to get out of the way quickly. Throughout his adult life Lipton, indubitably born in Glasgow, would be referred to as Irish. American magazines and newspapers were inclined to go into rhapsodies about his soft Irish brogue, although that did not prevent the occasional individualist or perhaps more perceptive reporter from commenting upon his pleasant Scottish burr.

The question of accent is important because throughout his life Lipton tended to be Scottish or Irish as the occasion demanded. This is not conjecture, we have his own words for it:- "When there is any argument as to my real nationality I come right into the open with the declaration that I am a Scottish-Irishman or an Irish-Scotsman, according to the leanings of the company I happen to be in at the moment!" One of his most valuable assets in his commercial and social life would be the ability to adapt, chameleon-like, to the company he happened to be keeping.

It is true that both parents were Irish, and Lipton himself claimed to be able to adopt any dialect within the British Isles for the purpose of greeting customers, but once again there is the strong probability that the accent of the street and the playground would prevail.

He was enrolled at the parish school of St. Andrew, adjoining Glasgow Green. Primary education was available and if not technically free the fee of threepence a week was not likely to threaten seriously even a budget as modest as the Lipton one.

There was a certain resistance from the young Crown Street boy to school and lessons. Reading between the lines he appears to have pulled against the collar and for a time was transferred to another, nameless, establishment. It is quite clear that eventually he made up his mind that school could teach him

Lipton's mother

things that might be useful, the three R's of course, but no sign is apparent of any attraction to things academic for their own sake. This may have merely betokened the strong pragmatic streak that was such a persistent feature of his character or he may have thought that since there was little financial chance of proceeding to further education it made more sense to cut his losses.

His mark at school, and remember we rely solely on his own account at this stage, was made in the field of extra-curricular activities. He describes himself as the ringleader of the local boys in all their pranks and ploys and highly active in the doings of their gang, the Crown Street Clan. The picture he wishes us to have is of a tall, well-set up boy who was far from belligerent but who could look after himself should war land on the doorstep. Two themes predominate in his relations of this time. One was his fight with Wullie, a butcher's son, known as the Bully of Crown Street. Wullie soon identified the organising Lipton as a likely rival and challenged him to a fight. A lesser man would have ended his story with Wullie receiving a hiding. Not Tom Lipton, he retired well-whipped after six rounds or so but not before he had inflicted such damage that the said Wullie let him severely alone in future.

Lipton appeared one day with a wooden boat which he himself had laboriously carved and rigged. Crown Street was then at the very edge of the expanding city and there were still green fields in plenty near the house. In one of these, the High Field, young Tom Lipton's first boat was launched and it was called, as so many of its successors would be, *Shamrock*. He and his friends formed a club which raced toy yachts on the dubbs or pools of the High Field and in Lipton's memoirs he was the Commodore.

He claimed that his childhood was idyllic and there is no reason to doubt that this was so. He had two loving parents who, although not the repressive Victorians of legend, were quite capable of severe reproof when he failed in his duty. Like many of his schoolmates he neither had any money nor felt the want of it but now coming up to eleven years of age, he was realising, again like so many of them, that it was time to leave school to begin his real education.

Lipton would always maintain that in the characters of his parents he had been given the best possible start in life. Curiously, another Scot who would be spectacularly successful in the United States and whom he would come to know well, Andrew Carnegie, said much the same thing. "I pity the sons and daughters of rich men who are surrounded by servants and governesses. They do not know what they have missed. They have fathers and mothers - very kind fathers and mothers too and they think they enjoy the sweetness of those blessings to the full but this they cannot do. For the poor boy who has in his father his constant companion, tutor and model and in his mother - holy name - his nurse, teacher, guardian angel, saint, all in one, has a richer and more precious fortune than any rich man's son can possibly know and compared with which all other fortunes count as little".

With those exalted and high-flown sentiments Lipton was in complete accord. The desire to repay his parents for their careful nurturing of him was deeply ingrained. He wanted to do what he could, as soon as he could, to ease their financial burden. The best way to achieve this, it seemed to him was to get a job and accordingly in November 1860 at the age of ten and a half years, young Thomas Lipton crossed the brown waters of the Clyde and set off to conquer Glasgow.

Lipton's birthplace.

CHAPTER 2
THE YOUNG MONEY-EARNER

It is tempting to see the young Lipton, trudging manfully off towards the city centre to seek gainful employment, as some kind of Dickensian waif about to be cruelly exploited. It is tempting, but quite erroneous. Young Tom Lipton was coming from a happy home which would be forever for him a sure and strong refuge and he was the most eager of volunteers.

He was not being snatched unwilling from school; on the contrary he was eager to be on with the real world and the great assets which he offered to the marketplace were a total commitment to hard work, a pleasing boyish personality and a great love of selling as theatre. Very early in life he coined one of his favourite maxims:- "Work is more fun than fun".

He had some small experience of selling. A couple of years beforehand his parents had opened a small semi-basement shop at 13 Crown Street from which they sold bacon, eggs and butter, relying on their Irish contacts for supplies. The goods came over on one of the flotilla of steamers that linked Scotland and Ireland at that time and the young boy earned his first pennies by wheeling a handcart down to the docks and collecting the produce there. The fact that a nine year old could bring the goods back to the shop unaided is an eloquent proof that the enterprise was small-scale.

The first indication of the boy's uncommon commercial shrewdness came at an early stage when he suggested to his father that the selling of eggs should always be left to his mother, as the eggs would look larger in her small delicate hands. From the very beginning selling for him was something not simply to do, but to think about.

He would not be a grocer straightaway, however; that would have been of no assistance to the family budget since the tiny shop could not have carried even his tiny wage.

He would say nothing of his intentions to his parents either, until he had landed a position for he did not wish them, especially his mother, to be arguing that he should stay on at school. He had thought about that as an option and discarded it. That day as he trudged the city centre, eyes scanning windows for the handwritten notice that might mean a vacancy, dodging the horse-buses and the heavy drays, he had already bade farewell to formal education. There would yet be a few skirmishes with it, half-hearted attempts to learn French and German, a handful of violin lessons, but these were simply tangential. He would teach himself henceforth.

A few years later, when elementary education became compulsory, he would have been hauled back to school by one of the truancy officers who rounded up delinquents. Life was simpler in the 1860s, the family was struggling, and as the small provision shop gave every sign of going under, well then, something had to be done.

In Glassford Street, a few hundred yards from Glasgow Cross, he found the notice he was looking for in the window of a shop, A. & W. Kennedy, Stationers. Was the job filled? No. Could he have it? Yes. When could he start? Immediately. In those few seconds Lipton and business became inextricably linked. As he had thought, his mother put up a token resistance but he knew how to talk her round. In a few days, his first wage, half-a crown, had been proudly deposited with her.

Whoever employed Thomas Lipton could be sure of attracting his best efforts. That did not mean that he was prepared to labour for long in what he perceived to be a dead-end job and in his judgement the Kennedy job was not demanding enough for a twelve-year old, let alone the adult he would one day be.

He therefore changed station and took up with Messrs. Tillie & Henderson of Miller Street, a stone's-throw away. He was paid almost twice as much, which was gratifying, but the job was almost twice as stultifying. In essence it consisted of nothing more than cutting out shirt patterns and making them up into sample books for the firm's commercial travellers.

A month or two was long enough to convince him that he had mastered all that the job required he knew and on the strength of this he was emboldened to ask for a 25% rise. The response was terse and emphatic. The cashier's note said "You are getting as much as you are worth and are in the devil of a hurry asking for a rise".

More than half a century later the chairman of Tillie & Henderson wrote a letter to Sir Thomas Lipton as he then was, stating that a young lady known to him was going out to Serbia with the next Red Cross party which the one-time sample-paster was taking there, although of course D.A. Sinclair, the chairman was totally ignorant of the coincidence. Mr. Sinclair requested that if Sir Thomas could show her any individual attention he would be most grateful. After reminding the embarrassed Mr. Sinclair that they had met before, Sir Thomas assured him he would do anything he could.

That was 1915, but in 1862 the refusal of his wage claim was a sign to the young Lipton that he would not be long with Tillie and Henderson. It was advisable to have another post in prospect before moving and by chance an opening came which not only doubled his weekly wage but was greatly to his liking, for the work was as a cabin-boy between Glasgow and Belfast with the Burns Line.

Over a century later it is almost impossible to visualise or imagine how busy the Irish trade was in the mid-Victorian years. The population of Glasgow doubled twice between 1830 and 1870 and many of the incomers were from Ireland. Ships ran nightly between Glasgow and Dublin, Glasgow and Belfast, Glasgow and Londonderry and there were rather less frequent connections with Waterford, Sligo, Limerick and Cork.

Major shipping lines abounded, the Anchor Line, the City Line, the Ellerman Line, the Henderson Line, the Clan Line, the Denholm Line, the Blue Funnel Line, a very litany of the sea. The Clyde built many of the ships that made the Atlantic the great motorway of the emigrants, steam had made passages predictable and increasingly affordable. At the very moment that he went to sea Clyde-built ships were acting as blockade-runners in a desperate attempt to prolong Southern resistance in the American Civil War.

The work on the passenger ferries of the Burns Line (later as the Burns Laird Line it would convey the Irish Sea traffic until well into the 1960s), was onerous and unremitting with only the shortest of turn-round times at either port. Yet for Lipton these were exalted days; he had always been keen on maps and read atlases as another might read a novel. All his life he was to be fascinated by faraway places and their inhabitants and on the boat he first met businessmen who operated on a considerable scale. He did not talk to them of course but he watched and

The Broomielaw , Glasgow.
Lipton departed from here on his voyage to America in 1865.

20

learned and harboured the desire to go much further afield. And yet, eight shillings was eight shillings!

The decision in the end was taken for him. On docking at Glasgow one morning the shore steward came on board on a routine tour of inspection. He was displeased to find that a cabin lamp had been allowed to smoke and so severely discoloured a cabin ceiling. The blame, at the telling of the Chief Steward fell on the luckless cabin boy and he was dismissed summarily.

The discharged mariner saw this as opportunity rather than catastrophe. Always he had given the bulk of his money to his mother, although he had contrived to save a little of his wage, and his willingness and outgoing personality meant that he was well and frequently tipped. It was time to see what lay behind the atlases. Rather apprehensively he informed his parents one night in the late winter of 1865 that he intended to take passage for the United States and after a long discussion his wishes prevailed.

Unselfishly and rather courageously the parents let the boy go, and he embarked on the unavoidably rugged steerage passage across the Atlantic.

He was in the company of whole families of Irish and Highlanders and although tall and well set-up for his age, he was almost as much child as youth. In later life his memory played him false and he would claim to have gone across on the Anchor liner Devonia, which in fact did not come into service until 1868.

The Belfast-Glasgow run, stormy more often than not, had made him a good sailor however and his cheerful optimism and willingness to undertake the writing of letters for those passengers who were not skilled in that department made him a natural leader. According to his own account he was first off the ship when it landed at Castle Gardens, New York and buttonholed one of the many boarding-house keepers who were looking for custom from the newly-arrived vessel. Selecting one whose face was a veritable map of Ireland, he enquired of him what concessionary rate he, Lipton, might expect if he introduced a dozen or so paying guests.

Lipton's skill in physiognomy was justified when Mike McCauligan of 27 Washington Street offered to put him up free for a week in that happy event. The young Scot, who tells us that at that moment he possessed a mere thirty shillings, (roughly eight dollars at the current rate of exchange) was happy to clinch the deal.

For once we can be fairly sure of dates here since Lipton definitely states that he celebrated his fifteenth birthday on American soil. If this is so then he must have landed in the weeks immediately after the surrender of the main Confederate Army under Robert E. Lee, at Appomattox to General Ulysses S. Grant.

In his book Lipton claims that there was no work to be had in New York or the surrounding district because of the influx of returning soldiers but the chronology would tend to indicate that he would have been in New York before the large-scale demobilisation of the Grand Army of the Republic. However that may be he took the offer of employment on a tobacco plantation in Dinwiddy County between the towns of Petersburg and Richmond in Virginia.

The state of Virginia had suffered more heavily than any other except South Carolina in the course of the war between the States and damage would have been widespread and evident. In any event the country was still occupied by Federal troops and would remain so for a couple of years but Lipton has nothing to say about it. When at the end of his time in Virginia he takes a brief trip round the state his reflections are vague in the extreme.

"..I spent a day or two at Virginia and visited the home of Jefferson Davis and the Hollowwood Cemetery. Young as I was I remember with what eagerness I visited all the historic spots around Virginia. It seemed to my mind that I was walking on holy ground indelibly associated with the glorious early romance of the vast new land, the new people and the new spirit amongst which I now found myself a very humble but admiring unit".

With his capacity to please, Lipton established good relations with his employer Sam Clay who looked after him when he had an accident with an axe which threatened one of his feet. The hard work in the tobacco fields helped to develop a powerful physique and inured him to hours of toil but there was no variety or real advancement in the job and he resolved to make another dart at New York.

What is faintly surprising is not that he should have had no luck a second time, for by this time the troops *were* back, but that he should decide to make a foray once more to the south. It must be emphasised how unusual a course of action this was. The vast majority of European immigrants came in at the big ports of Boston, New York, Philadelphia or Baltimore and either stayed in the north-east or at once set out west. Almost without exception they avoided the southern states for two reasons. The first was that they were not industrial and therefore could not provide jobs in numbers. The second and more important reason was that since the abolition of slavery in 1863 in the Confederate States, black freed men could be got to work for very little and therefore white immigrants did not wish to be forced into a Dutch auction for their labour.

Lipton's second trip to the South was to the state that had suffered most at the hands of General William Sherman, South Carolina. Here he worked on a rice plantation - the state's most important product - at Coosaw Island, up near the Georgia state line.

It was here that he had the adventure with the Spaniard which came near to blighting his life. The Spaniard was his landlord and had been stationed at Fort Sumter during the Civil War, self-evidently therefore he had fought on the Confederate side. Although married by then he had fallen in love with a Charleston girl and whenever he could still corresponded with her although himself almost a non-writer. Perhaps the young Scot would write a letter for him to his girl?

The young Scot did, presumably under dictation and put the envelope in his jacket ready for posting where it was discovered by the wife who had become suspicious on seeing Lipton and the Spaniard go off into the woods. She produced the letter and challenged her husband with it and he, furious at what he took to be betrayal by his lodger, went for Lipton with a knife.

"Before I realised what was happening he had drawn a knife from his belt and slashed me across the face with it. Only my agility and fleetness of foot prevented me from being murdered. He pursued me all the way to the overseer's house. Fortunately Mr. Mathews, the overseer was on the spot and he not only dressed my wounds but held off the Spaniard with a loaded revolver".

If he had been slashed across the face with a knife why were there no lasting scars? Were there lasting scars and was his luxuriant moustache his device for concealing them?

At all events relations were restored with the Spaniard and his senora and Lipton continued to live with them. He remained at Coosaw Island largely because he was allowed to take over in the plantation office with responsibility for the financial running of the establishment and the keeping of the books. This gave him a good grounding in how an enterprise was run and was a practical rehearsal for his future career in a way which no amount of night classes could have been. Before long however, he had extracted all the useful experience that such a job was likely to provide and it was time to be on the road once more.

His decision to go was swift and sudden and his departure took place under cover of night. The offending Spaniard woke to find that his canoe had been borrowed to take Lipton and an unnamed companion out to a schooner bound for Charleston.

The next two years appear to drift by in a veil of imprecise recollection and read like one of the boys' books popular at the time, such as R.M. Ballantyne's *Coral Island*. Sometimes he is lucky as when he arrives in Charleston in the wake of a major fire and is enlisted in the Fire Corps at the giddy but short-lived rate of fifty cents a day. He is doing what would now be called "going on the road", from time to time going back to New York to see if things had picked up there and then plunging off once more into rural America.

The most improbable of his temporary jobs was his engagement as a tram-car operator in New Orleans which provided him in later life with one of the couthy stories he so loved to tell. He had a splendid landlady who looked after him well and whose pancakes were exceptional. Forty years on and now staying at the St. Charles Hotel in New Orleans he is informed that a lady wishes to see him and this is none other than his former landlady. The story is almost certainly true for Lipton had the great qualities of rarely forgetting a face and never forgetting a kindness.

At length New York yielded to the assiduous besieger and at a stroke Lipton knew what the rest of his life held for him. His description is characteristically imprecise: "I returned to New York where I was fortunate in obtaining a post as an assistant in a prosperous grocery store."

The nervous vitality of New York City never failed to have a tonic effect on Lipton. In his eightieth year he would contemplate yet another visit to the great town with the very keenest anticipation. Here he now learned the grocery trade and fell in love with the theatricality of the American way of selling, the hustle of salemanship which nevertheless did not exclude a general wish to give value for money. Of the two great American advertising slogans of the time, Lipton totally disregarded the one which said that if a man built a better mousetrap, though he lived in the depths of the forest the world would beat a path to his door.

For Lipton, the possession of a good product did not begin to be enough. The world had to know about it also. The other jingle then current in the USA was more to his taste:-

The man who on a trade relies must either bust or advertise

He came to see that shops must be scrupulously clean and well-lit. They had rarely been so in his native Glasgow. There were certain errors to be avoided of which the chief was the disappointment of a customer by not having an item in stock. The produce should be displayed in such a way that the housewife coming into the shop for the purchase of two articles should be so seduced by elegant presentation and competitive prices that she might well depart with half a dozen or more.

There was another notice in the New York grocery store which appealed to him. It said laconically "In God we trust, all others pay cash." He made up his mind that there would be no credit given in any shop he might own and at a stroke the potential burden of bad debt was removed.

In some respects Lipton's is an atypical success story. Most of the men who became millionaires in the United States in the middle to late nineteenth century had much of the buccaneer about them. They felt themselves bound to no man nor accountable to Government, attitudes best illustrated perhaps by Cornelius Vanderbilt's testy reply when warned that a contemplated course of action risked infringing the law:- "Law? What do I care about the law? Hain't I got the power?"

By contrast Lipton for long reaches of time seemed ultra-cautious. His foot never left the rock-face unless his handhold was assured. Throughout his career he stayed well within the law, indeed he was astonishingly law-abiding for a man in the process of acquiring a huge fortune.

He had however the knack of occasionally going off in a totally unexpected direction and this he did in the spring of 1869. He was valued in the New York shop, he was learning well and fast the essentials of the provision trade and the normal path of development would have led him to open up for himself in a small way either in New York itself or in another of the dozen or so industrial cities which now dotted the east coast in a chain. Instead, in the spring of 1869 he decided to re-cross the Atlantic and try his luck once more in his native city.

Why would he opt to do this? In his adopted country he had everything going for him. He had a prodigious appetite for work. He was athletically-built, good-looking and had very taking manners. He was white, Protestant and English-speaking. From his earlier travels in the United States he had a profound knowledge of "real America" which was denied to nineteen out of twenty immigrants. Men without a quarter of his advantages would in the next few years do very well indeed in the States and there is no reason whatever to doubt that Lipton could have equalled or indeed eclipsed their achievements.

Nevertheless he chose to return. Perhaps he realised that the modern methods he so much admired in New York would inevitably be fairly standard practice in the urban United States whereas they would fall on Glasgow with all the shock and delight of novelty. More probably he felt bound by the promise he had made his mother to return at some stage and the time was now right. He had managed to save £100, by no means a negligible sum, and his parents were by now well into their sixties. He therefore reversed the current trend and took an east-bound ship from New York in the spring of 1869, an assured young man who had no tinge of arrogance, and whose willingness to believe the best of the world concealed just a tinge of naivete.

He landed early on a Saturday morning, bearing gifts and mementoes of his sojourn abroad. Chief among these were a barrel of flour and a rocking-chair for his mother, both long-promised. As with so many presents the symbolism far outweighed the monetary value of the gifts. The landing was an opportunity for the young Lipton to demonstrate his newly-acquired talents for showmanship. Not for him the early-morning return through empty streets and the unloading of his booty before a gallery of one cab driver. He deferred his departure from the docks until early afternoon - most industrial workers worked a long half-day on Saturdays then - and timed his arrival at Crown Street to coincide with the return of the men from the factories and the yards.

In a smart hired carriage he swept along Crown Street, rocking-chair and flour barrel precariously but ostentatiously lashed to the roof. He describes his return in the following terms:

"I told the driver to proceed to the end of Crown Street and then drive slowly through that thoroughfare. My plan could not have worked better. Leaning out of the cab I saluted all my friends with a shout and a cheery wave of the hand. Thus my return caused quite a sensation among my friends".

There is a charming ingenuousness in the assumption that each neighbour in Crown Street would be unfeignedly glad to see Mr. Lipton return "wi' muckle silver an' goold" as his father had predicted four years beforehand. Back he was and the stage was set for the ex-Commodore of the Crown Street Yacht Club to take the first steps in his plan to revolutionise totally the retail grocery industry. Those of his friends who remembered him - and four years is a long time at that stage in life - would already have thought that he had done well enough. His mother, to whom he had confided his future projects, knew that he had not begun to operate to anything like his full potential.

Thomas Lipton, aged 27.

CHAPTER 3
BRANCHING OUT

In a very real sense young Thomas Lipton, now fast approaching twenty years of age, was pretty well much where he had been before setting off for the United States. Certainly he had gathered £100, a far from negligible sum then, and he had proved that he could subsist on his own in alien surroundings but as he took over his parents' shop and swiftly began to turn its precariously-balanced finances round, it became ever more apparent to him that this state of affairs did not begin to offer a satisfactory permanent outcome.

The first pictorial advertisement utilized by Lipton.

THE FIRST PICTORIAL ADVERTISEMENT UTILIZED BY LIPTON

The main reason for this was the very different cast of mind of Old Tom and Young Tom. The son had seen what American drive and imagination could do and was desperate to introduce such methods here. He knew about them from first hand, his potential competitors could not possibly know. To him it was folly to pour out one's energies in a small and totally insignificant shop when there were vast worlds to conquer. He must control not only the supply of goods but, in so far as he could, their means of production also. He was convinced that he could make twice as much from two shops and more than quadruple his profits from four. For him the enlargement of the business was a welcome challenge which given his own enthusiasm and infinite capacity for hard work was bound to bring results.

The father looked at things differently. Where the son saw increased opportunity for profit the father could see nothing but increased responsibility which he did not seek. To have his one little shop afloat and doing modestly well was fully to meet his undemanding expectations. He said as much when the returned emigrant raised yet again the question of expansion and he used a homely Ulster metaphor. "Ah, no Tom, we'd be getting above ourselves. The neighbours would say that the peas were getting above the sticks."

The young man tried to convince his father by firm argument, to coax him and once to threaten him with a fait accompli. From nowhere one morning a frisky little horse arrived, its harness as gleaming as the van it pulled was fresh-painted. On each side it bore the single word LIPTON. The old man enquired where this smart turn-out had come from and his son admitted, half-proudly, half-shyly, that he had ordered it for the business. Lipton senior would have none of it and instructed that the equipage be returned. It mattered not that the younger man had not only ordered the horse and van but had paid for it. It mattered not that its arrival had created more public interest in Crown Street than any other happening there in months.

Lipton took the horse and vehicle back to the firm from which he had ordered it. He told the firm to regard it as only an order deferred for the incident had made up his mind. His father would not alter and he was too fond of his parent to press his own views over-strongly on him. Besides, he had a shrewd suspicion that his mother was on his side; she had always been the more venturesome of the two with a better head for money.

He had worked hard in the little shop for his parents, nobody could accuse him of any dereliction of duty. He had now to move on. The young man was convinced that a major secret in being a successful businessman was the ability to spot a good opportunity and then, equally important, to have the nerve and decision to act. He had recently put this to the proof when on an instant, walking along the Glasgow docks, he came upon a ship which had made very heavy weather of a Philadelphia crossing and comfortably missed her arrival date. In consequence her cargo was being sold off piecemeal. He bought a couple of score hams, trailed them round the small grocers of the South Side and cleared eighteen pounds on the deal. If you could do that on forty hams or so, what might be done with two thousand?

Mrs. Lipton was by now determined to let her son have his way and with what he still had from the U.S.A., his recent profit and approximately £60 lent by his parents he was ready to strike out on his own. At £100 the venture was assuredly not over-capitalised but it would be headed by a man who could daily do the work of three. He had earmarked a shop in Stobcross Street in Anderston, on the north bank of the river and with a precise sense of timing it opened to the public on the proprietor's 21st birthday, May 10th 1871.

Before he served his first customer he had secured his supply lines in the best military tradition. He had a little network of suppliers in Ireland which was merely an augmentation of the contacts who had kept the Crown Street shop going. From the start he paid out cash on the nail and as comparatively few retailers did this he immediately got into the good graces of the Irish side of the operation.

Stobcross Street was in the heart of industrial Glasgow, the smoky streets of Anderston filled with the clamour of works' hooters and those of the ships on the Clyde. Chimneys belched smoke even in summer and in winter thick industrial fog could hang about murkily for days. The new shopowner was determined that in this dingy background his premises would be literally and metaphorically a shining light. He would always be dressed from top to toe in white, and as the business grew, so too would his staff. His shops would be brilliantly, almost exaggeratedly lit, first with gas and later with "the electric" as it was at first known.

Lipton's first shop in Stobcross Street, Glasgow.

It was a one-man enterprise. Like Gilbert and Sullivan's First Lord of the Admiralty Lipton "cleaned the windows and he scrubbed the floor and he polished up the handle of the big front door". The new shop was his baby and he welcomed the quiet periods when he could get outside to wipe the already-clean windows or burnish the brass still brighter. This gave him the chance to chat with passing housewives and draw attention to special offers.

Not that there were many quiet periods. His keen pricing saw to that with ham as little as 5d per lb. and top quality ham at 7d. One of the first things he had to learn was that top price, even in his cheap range, required top quality. Buying intelligently and honestly was crucial. A favourite saying of his was "Well bought is half sold".

He was a human whirlwind. His day started by his pushing a cart down to the quay where the Irish boats arrived with the frequency of present-day city buses. There he loaded up with his purchases, got back to Stobcross Street, dressed the windows, ticketed the produce, delivered any orders that might be outstanding in those first few weeks, balanced the books and then at the end of what was never less than an 18 hour day fell asleep. As often as not he did not make the 20 minute walk home across the river but slept on a makeshift bed underneath the counter.

What for others would have been an existence of quite intolerable drudgery was for him a life of the keenest joy. He was doing what he loved best, selling, and furthermore for the first time in his life he was working for his own hand. Quite soon his first important decision awaited him. The Stobcross Street shop was doing so well that it seemed foolish not to follow his own dictum and acquire another. The snag was that not even the Herculean young Scot could supervise two stores simultaneously and adequately.

He acquired his first assistants simply by hunch and claimed rarely to have been deceived. His method was simplicity itself: identify a likely young fellow among the thousands bustling to work each Glasgow week-day, enquire how much he earned in his present employment, offer to double the sum and then see how things went.

In some respects Lipton gives a strong impression of having something of the frustrated actor in him. Certainly he believed that the prosaic act of shopping ought to become something more of a theatrical experience and he makes a fair claim to having been the Phineas T. Barnum of the retail grocery trade. Always keenly alive to the possibilities of graphic reproduction, at an early stage he engaged the services of Willie Lockhart, a noted cartoonist who within a few months made the name of Lipton known all over Scotland.

When we look at the simplistic, rudimentary cartoons which Lockhart did for Lipton it has to be borne in mind that both men were breaking new ground. In a few lines Lockhart would create a coil of lugubrious skeletal figures who were according to the caption GOING TO LIPTON'S and on the next page a gaggle of plump Pickwickians whose beaming faces attested that they were COMING FROM LIPTON'S. This basic idea was cleverly used at a higher social stratum when in the late 1870's the members of a defeated Cabinet were seen slouching along in a melancholy fashion until on the next page they returned clutching dripping hams and large eggs as ample consolation for their rejection at the polls. Where had they been? By now it was not even necessary to ask.

"What's the matter with the pig, Pat?"
"Sure, Sirr, he's an orphan so, out of pity, I'm taking him to Lipton's!"

One of the earliest cartoons displayed in Lipton's shop.

His use of advertising was simple, clever and effective. No use advertising in a city newspaper when as yet he had but one shop. Handbills had been invented for this purpose. But there were many grocer's shops and most of them had handbills. How to stand out, how to be the firm that was talked about? Something was needed to set tongues wagging outside the shop. From this cogitation came the notion of Lipton's Orphans. In essence this required the services of a "stage Irishman" in cutaway coat, billycock or stovepipe hat and kneebreeches, of the kind familiar from such Victorian melodramas as *The Shaughraun* or *The Colleen Bawn*. The Orphans were two fat pigs who were led through the streets by said Irishman to the shop before they continued to their earthly terminus. People loved it, children followed behind like a screeching swarm of insects and Glasgow on its collective way to work stopped and smiled for a moment and enquired the name of the impresario. The idea of course was that the pigs were orphans because Lipton had already acquired the rest of the porcine family and bringing in these two stragglers could therefore be construed as an act of philanthrophy.

It was a pleasant idea for the time and capable of unexpected spin-offs. Quite by accident one day the leading rope broke and the pigs, sensing a last-minute reprieve, turned themselves loose into the traffic, causing much confusion, annoyance to those charged with maintaining the flow of traffic and considerable hilarity among those watchers who had no objection to seeing their officials and police thus discomfited. Strangely, from then on for the next few weeks every other pig delivered seemed to have a frayed leading-rope.

Nowadays, with marketing brought to almost an exact science, it is difficult to imagine just how non-visual retailing then was. When Lipton swung a painted ham above his shop door in Stobcross and the newly-painted object began to run in the sun, the reaction was electric. People came from all over Anderston to see "the dripping ham".

It is not enough to have good ideas. The real genius will know when these have run their course and will take care that they do not overstay their welcome. Lockhart was endlessly inventive, to the extent that people would make detours to see what the day's cartoon was. An especial favourite showed an enormous policeman collapsing into a large basket outside a hen-house with the caption "Great fall in eggs!"

It was now that Lipton, always anxious to maximise the talent of his employees in the service of the firm, discovered that his cartoonist, Lockhart, possessed another but equally striking aptitude. He was a butter sculptor of a very high order and this was an art highly prized in Glasgow shops. The author remembers being awe-struck as a child when he saw the manager of one of the Maypole shops sculpting a marvellous thistle and lion rampant on the tops of two majestic butter tubs.

Lockhart was even more adept than that and among his productions he re-introduced his fat policeman, to whom he seemed to have taken an individual dislike, with a beautiful dairymaid regarding the constable with disdain from the other side of a stile.

There was always something doing in Lipton's shop. It might be the concave mirror which greeted customers at the door, rendering them gaunt, haggard, pinched. Often people would almost be unable to enter the shop for laughing. As they left convex mirrors would render them fat, jolly and contented. Nothing like it had been seen in Scotland and the little enterprise thrived. Its owner was in love with his work and a seemingly unending stream of novel ideas flowed from him.

He had always intended to open other shops in Glasgow but his original ambitions had stopped there. Had he remained of that opinion he would have enjoyed a local reputation, nothing more. Glasgow was well served by "ham and egg shops", the names of Curley, McGlinchey and K.P. Keane prominent in various districts of the city. As Lipton tells it a bizarre happening led him to think of extending his empire beyond Clydeside.

He had engaged a German, Herr Schultz, to teach him the rudiments of that language but the latter had failed to show up although he had not omitted to collect payment in advance. Attempts to persuade Herr Schultz to discharge his part of the bargain having proved futile, Lipton was eventually moved to call upon him - with a typically vague Lipton touch in such stories the house was "somewhere in the neighbourhood of St. Vincent Street" - and exact physical retribution.

The offended German then sought police assistance and Lipton was compelled to flee from Jerusalem to Jericho or at any rate from Glasgow to Dundee. While there he saw a shop in Murraygate which he determined to make the site of the first expansion of his empire beyond his native city. He was able to make his exile a short one because Herr Schultz attracted the interests of the Glasgow Police who charged him with several frauds and misdemeanours.

Here again the careful reader will say "perhaps". Is it possible that what was very much a one-man operation could do without its mainspring for even a week? Would he go to such lengths, being a realistic man, to recover a few shillings or their equivalent in punches? And although police work was comparatively rudimentary in the early 1870s, Glasgow to Dundee was not exactly Seattle to Samarkand. More probably Lipton would have come to realise that although the acquisition of German was desirable in the abstract, the mastery of it would have acquired a totally disproportionate amount of time and energy at that stage of his career.

In any event the Dundee shop was in the future and for the moment he had two new Glasgow shops to see to, one in the High Street and one in Jamaica Street, two of the busiest thoroughfares in town. It is interesting to note that although these were two much better pitches, the principles on which he ran the new shops were exactly the same as those he had applied in Stobcross Street. His target was as ever the respectable working class; he had no aspirations to move up market, to be ranked with Fortnum and Mason. That would come much later if it came at all.

There is no need to set down the detail of each addition to his chain of shops. It is enough to say that within five years of opening in Stobcross Street there were twenty shops throughout the west of Scotland which traded under the name of Lipton. How to keep the impetus up, how to keep his name before the public?

Part of the answer lay in his own honesty of approach. He bought as well as he could as cheaply as he could. When a new shop opened he made a point of serving the first half-dozen or so customers in person and as his fame grew so too did the value of this ploy. In the entire span of his career he never felt that he had grown beyond the serving of customers.

The remainder of the answer lay in his catherine wheel of a mind. He was always quick to borrow the bons mots of other people although to do him credit he rarely tried to pass them off as his own. A throw-away remark by Gladstone in a political speech in Glasgow had impressed him greatly. "Nothing except the Mint can make money without advertising".

By this time he and his parents were living in Cambuslang, some five miles to the east of Glasgow. Cambuslang was a peculiar place, its lower area was filled with mean tenements which confronted steel mills and chemical works but up the hill there lay street upon street of handsome stone-built Victorian houses and, the part triumphing over the whole, it was known as "the villa village".

By now the scale of the operation demanded a huge depot or warehouse at Lancefield Street in Finnieston, literally within yards of where the Irish boats docked. He was on course for his dream. He had been able to provide handsomely for his parents and they lived with him, although they probably saw no more of him than anyone else, such were the demands of his work. His mother had the horse and carriage that he had always promised her and the days of struggle in the half-basement shop seemed like a period spent in another existence.

Glasgow, Greenock, Paisley, Aberdeen, the roll lengthened. When asked what his politics were - it was now worthwhile to learn what this rising young man thought - he deftly turned the question with a smiling "My politics are to open a new shop every week". Throughout his life he would have the talent to deflect and defuse questions which might wrong-foot him without offending the questioner.

COMING FROM LIPTON   GOING TO LIPTON

Had Lipton been a musician his favourite form of composition might well have been Theme and Variations. He had an uncanny faculty for not only producing bright ideas but going on to further develop them. A good example of this was his brilliant use of giant cheeses. In 1881 he informed the breathless citizens of Glasgow that he intended to bring to the city the greatest cheese ever made. Knowing the public's reverence for statistics he let it be known that 800 cows had required to be milked for six days and that the labour of 200 dairymaids had been necessary to make this great cheese in Whiteborough, New York.

One of the earliest Lipton advertisements displayed in his shops. These cartoons were altered week by week and people flocked from all over Glasgow to see them.

When the cheese arrived at the Glasgow docks thousands gaped at it as a steam traction-engine inched it through the streets. Lipton took care to make its positioning in the shop-window as protracted and dangerous as possible and once safely installed it drew huge crowds for several weeks afterwards.

A good idea invoked a better. Why not insert twenty or thirty half-sovereigns throughout the cheese in the way that Scots had traditionally baked threepenny pieces in their clootie dumplings? No sooner thought than executed and for once it looked as if an idea of his might well be far too successful for its own good. A huge crowd descended on the shop and bought large hunks of cheese, tearing it apart in their haste to find out if luck was theirs. The handful of police were powerless but

35

fortunately the prevalent atmosphere was good-humoured and in any event the cheese had melted like May snow within a couple of hours.

Use the cheese idea again but vary it. What else could convey it besides a steam engine? An elephant could, if there happened to be a circus in town. If there were not then dress up fifty men as coolies and have them drag it through the streets with ropes. Make the cheeses bigger, five tons and beyond. If a University town was having a rag week make use of it, have the students "dissect" the great cheese as in an operating theatre. Novelty and the chance of winning a sovereign would do the rest.

Lipton had a genius for counter-propaganda. When he moved south of the border and opened up in the north-east of England he was of course dealing with a different legal system. Thus the operation seemed to be thwarted in Sunderland when the local authorities held that it must be construed as a lottery since there were money prizes to be won. Thinking on his feet Lipton discovered that he would be all right if he warned purchasers of the cheese that any money so gained must be returned at once. To nobody's very great surprise none of the winners who emitted strangled shouts of triumph felt themselves constrained to return anything they might have won.

Along the road in Newcastle, the objection was on a slightly different basis, namely the danger that in the rush and excitement of the day members of the public might well swallow one of the coins secreted within. For Lipton it was the work of half an hour to draft a notice for the bill-boards warning that anyone who bought a portion of his cheese was in grave danger of choking on the liberal supply of half-sovereigns seeded throughout the said cheese. Again, and predictably, this seemed to be a risk gladly run by the citizens of Newcastle-on-Tyne. At other times a prominent local or national personality might be invited to "cut ye up wi' ready slicht".

Just occasionally the sheer exuberance of the young merchant ran away with him rather. He had the quaint notion of issuing "One Pound Notes" which on closer inspection promised merely to supply one pound's worth of ham, butter and eggs on payment of fifteen shillings. At once, with the perennial optimism of Glaswegians, dozens of people emerged who claimed to have been duped by this issue, and to have suffered financial loss accordingly. This might just have been awkward in an age when a perceptible number of people still did not read easily if at all but what it needed was a convincing victim. As it happened the man who came to court was Francis McConnal, a clerk, and if he could not tell the difference between Lipton

Lipton's one pound note.

and the Bank of Scotland then his clerkly skills were indeed highly suspect.

In all this there was the occasional warning, even hectoring note from those who would not have been too reluctant to see the onward rush of the new Merchant of Glasgow at least temporarily checked. The *Glasgow Evening Citizen* of April 24th 1877 raised its voice in magisterial reproof. Referring to the issue of the Lipton pound notes it had this to say: "the danger of confusion, though comparatively small is something Mr. Lipton has found to his cost, and we believe he has done all in his power to recall the perilous documents".

The reference to costs was made because although the clerk Francis McConnal lost his case nevertheless Lipton was not able to recover costs. In fairness it has to be said that unfamiliar notes were even more vigorously scrutinised then than they would be today. The *Daily Mail* of May 29th 1877 had an article on the difficulty a traveller had experienced in changing Clydesdale Bank notes in Aberdeen.

When he eventually did open in Dundee in July 1877 it was on a large scale. The shop had 12 salesmen and three cash boys. Keen to keep the fires stoked Lipton let it be known that this meant that in a week his shops went through 6,000 hams, 16 tons of bacon, 16,000 dozen eggs and 10 tons of butter. His main Irish agency at this time was at Westport in County Mayo, where his involvement gave a perceptible lift to the economy of an impoverished county struggling still to recover from the worst effects of the Famine.

Lipton of course was much more than a dewy-eyed sentimentalist. He was tremendously proud of his Irish ancestry and whenever and wherever he could he would extend a helping hand to anybody from Ireland. This did not mean suspending his business acumen or critical faculties when dealing with that island. In August 1878 in a letter to the *Freeman's Journal* he told Irish butter producers quite bluntly that they would have to improve their standards of cleanliness and packaging or else lose out to Europe.

What seemed to have intrigued the outside world most in his early days was the scale of his involvement with the ham and bacon trade. Reference has already been made to Lipton's Orphans and the popular Glasgow magazine *The Bailie* continued on this theme with its assertion that "Mr. Lipton is a very Herod among the piggiwigs". With this staple of the provision trade it seemed that he could do no wrong; all his interventions prospered. If a man and his wife went to a music hall in the winter of 1879, say the Argyle Theatre of Varieties in Govan, they could hear the following song, by James Willison, Glasgow's favourite comedian and mime, as Mr. Willison modestly styled himself:

Lipton's butter, cheese and ham
That's the stuff for you to cram
Swallow his eggs and you'll stand on your pegs
Till you're as auld as Methusalam"

Closer inspection of the programme would have revealed that it was Mr. Willison's benefit night and that among the prizes donated for the Grand Draw to help the proceeds of the benefit was a ham from the same Mr. Lipton. Always the one hand washed the other. When the Aberdeen shop was opened in January 1883 a 20 pound ham was promised to the first customer and this happened, genuinely enough, to be a poor widow.

There were songs about him in Aberdeen too. Robert Vokes, an artiste appearing at McFarlane's Varieties and Music Hall in that city, was the proud originator of this ditty:

"Can anyone tell me where Lipton's is,
now would you be so kind as to tell me where his place is,
for him I want to find?
I want to go for I've wasted so I scarce know what I'm at,
And if I can find where Lipton's is he's sure to make me fat."

He was becoming very wealthy and highly successful. Just how successful he was was perhaps not known to most of his fellow-countrymen but if they did not comprehend the extent of his achievement the Americans did. In an article of February

Opposite. Unilever Archives.

39

1886 The *American Dairyman* said: "The salient feature of Mr. Lipton's character is enterprise. He has what is known in this country as nerve, supported by a calm judgement.... He seems to have picked up the Yankee habit of letting people know he has something to sell and as a result he is now one of the merchant princes of the world."

Even at this early age, in his mid-thirties, he could have retired very comfortably and been at least a local magnate of some consequence. Had he been a political animal this might indeed have been a possibility but he did not get sucked into politics, local or national, as so many Victorian merchants did. He did not lack invitations to stand for Parliament in both the Conservative and Liberal interests and such approaches would become more frequent and pressing as his career progressed. He may have been unwilling to take the risk of alienating a large section of his customers which any open declaration of allegiance might entail. It is far more probable that he simply found business a much more alluring and profitable career.

Occasionally he permitted himself what might have been an unguarded comment, but this was always humorously wrapped. In the great parade of floats through Glasgow in 1884 to campaign for the passage of the Third Reform Bill which was to bring universal manhood suffrage, Lipton had two carts in the procession. The first had a man dressed as William Gladstone, the Grand Old Man of British politics, who doffed his hat politely and waved decorously to the crowd. Immediately behind was a wagonload of black pigs which bore the legend on its side "The House of Lords - we'll cure 'em!" Perhaps from this grew the bizarre notion which persisted well into the 1890s, especially when the firm moved headquarters to London, that there was no such person as Thomas Lipton and that the company was really a front for the prominent Home Rulers of the time, Charles Stewart Parnell, Dillon and Biggart.

The normal pattern for such a man would have been that of unostentatious but steady local advancement. He might well have bought a yacht with the superb waters of the Clyde estuary on his doorstep. In Scotland he would almost certainly have tried to join one of the many golf clubs which were beginning to surround Glasgow as the railways pushed out. He might have become a patron of the arts or a subscriber to the national orchestra that one day might be more than a pipedream. He did none of these things. The business was still all-absorbing because he was for ever breaking new ground.

And not only in Scotland or, for that matter, even in Britain. He had long since realised that given the growth rate which he projected for his enterprise, Britain or even Europe would be unable to offer a guaranteed source of supplies for his grocery shops. Only the United States could do that, and not even for his beloved United States would he abandon his creed of abolishing the middleman.

In 1885 he founded the Johnstone Packing Company in Chicago, the title was taken from his own middle name. He felt that it was impossible to build the custom-built plant that he would need, together with unfettered access by rail. He therefore moved the operation to a small town in Nebraska, Omaha, where he soon became the major employer and in future years would actually claim credit for the settlement of the town. The Omaha venture flourished until in 1897 the operation moved back to Chicago where Lipton's became an incorporated company.

The Cork Packing House as it was known was a modern plant with the facility to kill and dress between 300 and 400 pigs a day. In *Leaves from the Lipton Logs* Lipton acknowledges the help he received from the already-established American leaders in the canned meat trade: "Here I would like to pay a tribute to the courtesy and goodwill extended to me at this crucial time in my life by my competitors in the pork-packing trade. Men of such weight and position as P.D. Armour, Louis Swift, Nelson Morris, John Hately and T.C. Boyd showed me immense kindness and the assistance they gave me kept me from making many blunders in a branch of business absolutely new to me and, as may well be imagined, studded with pitfalls for the unwary newcomer."

Why should these men have been so helpful to a newcomer, and a foreigner at that, in possibly the most cut-throat era ever of capitalist competition? Lipton at that time was a comparative unknown in the United States. Why help an unknown stranger? Was the agreement that Lipton would not seek to trade as a retailer on that side of the water? Such a deal seems unnecessary as with their collective muscle the American giants could have easily squeezed him out.

Just possibly the answer was his own boundless enthusiasm and genuine affability. He quotes an (unattributed) compliment from one of the pork kings relayed to him much later by the hog monarch's daughter:

"Do I remember Tommy Lipton sitting-in at the pork-packing game in Chicago?

I'll say I do! Till I met him I always thought that your Britisher was slow to get a move on at anything but this Lipton guy quickly knocked THAT notion for nix. Why, he just shooted around like an express train so that none of us ever saw him for more than ten seconds at a time!"

41

It was Lipton's belief that no doors were ever closed for long to the man of genuine goodwill. On a trip to the United States he managed to wangle an introduction to the then President, Rutherford Hayes, and although not a fanatical tee-totaller himself he was sufficiently one that he would have approved of Mrs. Hayes who in barring alcohol from the White House earned for herself the title of "Lemonade Lucy". Later in the first 30 years of the twentieth century there would hardly be a President with whom he was not at least on nodding terms.

He did not forget his origins. In his home village of Cambuslang in early 1887 he sent a letter to Samuel Colville, president of the Miners' Committee, enclosing a ten guinea cheque for the striking miners and more usefully, a strongly-worded message of support:- "I consider it a disgrace to a civilised country that men should be found doing a hard day's work and risking lives all for the miserable pittance presently earned. I am of the opinion that the miners are the worst-paid and most ill-treated class of men in Europe".

This was not the first time that he had expressed strong support, moral and financial for the colliers and the great British Labour leader, Keir Hardie would pay warm tribute to the generous and private expressions of support which had come from Thomas Lipton.

By now the remarkable improvement in late Victorian transport had inspired Lipton to look abroad for areas of expansion. Later, foreign travel would come to fascinate him for its own sake but at this stage the new countries were frankly so many business opportunities. Russia was fast opening up and the Industrial Revolution had arrived some sixty years after it had affected western Europe. The great empire proved an illusion however. Lipton landed a contract to provision the massive Russian Army but the deal foundered on the shoals and hidden reefs of Russian bureaucracy and Lipton expressed himself the least surprised man in Europe when confronted with the events there in 1917.

That was well in the future. Back in 1888 the country was gearing up for the Queen's Jubilee. Victoria had gone through all the stages, from girl-queen to mother of the family to a widow who had seemed to protract her reclusive grief almost to an undutiful degree. Now slowly she had come back to public life and there were stirrings of popular affection for her.

Her subjects dutifully offered gifts, and in the case of Thomas Lipton, inaptly so. The first sentence reads weirdly even across the years.

Opposite. Lipton in America.

"I take the liberty of writing to enquire whether Your Most Gracious Majesty would be pleased to accept of the largest cheese ever made. The cheese which I propose presenting to Your Majesty as a Jubilee offering would weigh about 11,200 pounds or not less than five tons and be made from one day's milk of 8,500 cows.

The cheese will be of the finest quality that can be manufactured. Your Majesty will readily understand that in order to make a cheese of this size, special machinery and plant are required; so that should Your Majesty be pleased to signify your gracious approval the necessary preparations will be happily and speedily gone on with.

I may mention that the cheese will be made in Canada; and I am sure Your Majesty's subjects there would be delighted with the additional opportunity thereby given them of showing their loyalty to Your Majesty while at the same time marking an event which has few parallels in the history of this or any other country. The cheese will be ready about September next.

Trusting sincerely that Your Majesty will accept what would be the most marvellous product of dairy enterprise of all ages, I have the honour to be Your Majesty's most humble servant."

The reply from the royal secretary, Sir Henry Ponsonby, was polite but icily formal. It simply said that Her Majesty was unable to accept presents from private individuals to whom she was not personally known. It would have been strange in other people, but perfectly in character for Thomas Lipton that he passed the correspondence to the press. He was not at all put out by a poem in *The Pioneer* which concluded with the stinging lines:- Snubbed by a Queen! Go, think of it in silence and shame And weigh against a piece of cheese The glories of a throne.

The story would not go away. Leaders of striking miners and wire-pullers wrote in to say that if the great cheese was not wanted at the Palace, their starving members and their families would be very glad of it. When the Diamond Jubilee came around in 1898 Lipton's approach would be more adroit and successful.

It would be so successful that it would catapult him to the heights of London society, win for him an hereditary dignity and make it no mere form of words to claim that he was on friendly terms with most of the royal personages of Europe. In the meantime, however, there remained a commercial empire to expand and the place for that expansion was increasingly beyond Britain.

It could fairly be said that Thomas Lipton's personal fortune was founded on butter, eggs and ham and that his going into the hog-dressing and killing business had made him fairly well-known in American business circles. The product that made him an international celebrity however was tea and his intervention in that area came at the end of the 1880s.

We are accustomed today to think of tea as a drink abundantly available to all classes but such was not the case barely a century ago. For working-class people the price of tea was prohibitive; tea which was not especially distinguished was selling at 3/4d per pound, a price well beyond the purses of labourers or artisans. Tea was a genteel drink. In John Galt's wonderful account of eighteenth century Lowland Scotland *The Annals of the Parish,* the Ayrshire minister, the Reverend Micah Balwhidder, rebukes his parishioners for the sin of tea-drinking for two reasons, firstly that the tea was smuggled and therefore the duty on it evaded, and secondly because ordinary folks had no claim to such luxuries.

Throughout the 1880s when Lipton was busily engaged opening shops all over the United Kingdom, he had been the subject of various approaches from the tea trade who saw the fast-growing chain of shops as an ideal outlet for their product. In this they did not know their man. Lipton would rarely evince any interest in a product unless he controlled the whole process from production of the raw material until packaging and final sale over the counter. The tea producers were confident that no outsider could break into an esoteric trade, particularly since he would totally lack the key men in the process, the blenders. Their confidence was misplaced.

In the summer of 1890 Lipton let it be known to the newspapers that he was contemplating a trip to Australasia with a view to opening some shops there. This seemed very plausible as the south-east of Australia became steadily more urbanised but neither Sydney nor Melbourne nor for that matter Adelaide was the intended destination. Lipton left the ship at Colombo, ostensibly for a few days stop-over, in reality to take the first steps that would make him pre-eminent in the tea trade and lead to all sort of puns on the Sir Tea Lipton lines. In a few years he and his great friend, the whisky magnate Tom Dewar, would be known simply as Whisky Tom and Tea Tom.

As in all his boldest strokes, and there was none bolder than this, his timing was immaculate. For a variety of reasons it was now possible to make the drink a universal beverage, no longer restricted to the gilded royalty of Pope's time;- "Here thou, great Anna, whom three realms obey Dost sometimes counsel take, and sometimes tea."

Chief among these reasons was the development of the Indian tea plantations - previously almost all of the tea consumed had originated in China. Less far to travel meant cheaper tea. So too did the increasing sophistication of steamships. The great China clipper races had been romantic and fascinating but above all uncertain; even such majestic vessels as the *Cutty Sark* were hostages to wind and weather.

Lipton's Dambattenne and Laymastotte tea factories, Ceylon.
Unilever Archives.

Lipton's bungalow in Ceylon.

Opposite.
Lipton at Mount Lavinia, Ceylon with U.S. Vice Consul, 1908.

There was a third reason. Just at this time land in Ceylon could be acquired at knock-down prices. Ceylon is now so indelibly associated with tea-production that it comes as a jolt to realise that until about 1870 it was thought of as primarily a coffee-producing island. When the coffee blight of 1878 virtually wiped out production of that commodity, tea-growing on the island stood at less than 20,000 lbs, annually. Before he had set foot in the eastern island Lipton had acquainted himself with this and any other useful information. The purchase price was barely half of what he had been prepared to pay.

Within a matter of months he owned five tea estates of which Dambutene, Oakfield and Monerakanda were the most important. There was also a rubber plantation, Keenapitya. Tea was, however, his great current interest and he had managed to acquire overall control of the manufacturing process. The insiders of the trade had proclaimed that he would be unable to operate without blenders and that he would be unable to procure these. Lipton was convinced that blenders were little different from the rest of the human race and that an offer of double their present salary would fall upon receptive ears. His assessment of human nature was as usual impeccable.

Given that he could control the production of the raw material, Lipton had always maintained that he could make a handsome profit by selling tea at 1/7d per pound - exactly half the going rate in the shops. He played up his ownership of the tea plantations for all it was worth. His tea would be brightly and individually packaged, not sold loosely in paper bags as often happened in England, or worse, left to stand in open barrels as was the case in the United States. He saw to it that drawings and photographs of the tea terraces, the factories and the sheds wherein dwelt the labour force were contained in each packet. There were attractive drawings of Cingalese girls, with the simple but effective slogan "Direct from the tea garden to the teapot".

He excelled at nothing more than planting in the public mind the idea that he was an astonishing innovator. Traditionally the workers had made their way down the steep terraces bearing heavy bags of newly-picked leaves on their backs, a task which was physically sapping and time-consuming. Lipton claimed to have originated a system whereby the tea sacks were shot down hill by a system of wires, rather as mail bags used to be collected by express trains at the track side. However, at least two other groups of tea plantations in Ceylon claimed to have introduced this improvement at this time.

Lipton had severely bruised the susceptibilities of the magnates of the tea trade. They had seen his shops as a profitable outlet but they now found that they had acquired a fierce competitor.

They did their best to rubbish the new entrant to the market but Lipton countered by offering a parcel of gold-tipped tea for public auction at Mincing Lane which went for thirty six guineas a pound.

Top. Loading the tea.
Unilever Archives.
Bottom. Lipton's tea gardens, Ceylon.
Unilever Archives.

Local transport, Ceylon.
Unilever Archives.

Armed with this ringing endorsement of his product he could afford to disregard a plaintive advertisement in the Newry newspaper in Ireland placed by Valentine and Company of Belfast. It offered £100 to the poor of Belfast if any of three experts to be appointed by a neutral panel could tell the difference between Valentine's 1/4d tea and Lipton's at 1/7d. But this time Lipton flexed his muscles and letters flew to several editors of several unimportant Irish local newspaper expressing strong surprise and disapproval at the mention of the name Lipton in Valentine's announcement and stating that if it recurred then all Lipton advertising in these newspapers would inevitably be withdrawn.

The expansion into tea was an enormous success. It allowed for the theatrical. Cargoes of tea were escorted from the docks by bands of so-called Cingalese musicians. Lipton acquired three servants from the island who would be with him until he died and, always a man for maximum mileage, jocularly remarked that he liked them because they reminded him of the advantages of "single ease" a reference to his continued bachelordom which by now was beginning to exercise the nation. He could afford to be philanthropic and gave tea away to deserving causes - striking miners, flood victims, the homeless.

*The earliest advertisement for
Lipton's tea.
Unilever Archives.*

In reality the bulk of his tea, which of course was blended, came from India and not Ceylon, but somehow he succeeded in achieving almost total identification with the island. This was not well received by the original planter class one of whom muttered that "he shouldn't be surprised to wake up one morning and find that the damn' place had been re-christened Liptonia."

His conquest of the British market was lightning-fast. The United States as usual would present a larger but potentially more lucrative challenge. He believed it was time that his beloved Yankees forgave and forgot the War of Independence and stopped drinking coffee as a political gesture. He knew from frequent visits to the Republic that American retailers knew nothing of the treatment or storage of tea. He was to make some little impact on the wealthy Anglophile upper class on the eastern seaboard - and there was an upper class despite flamboyant Yankee protestations of total democracy - but there was a cultural reservation involved and the U.S.A. proved as resistant to tea as the British Isles did to coffee.

51

He was to find another use for Ceylon, namely as an exotic location in which to entertain the distinguished people who were beginning to crowd into his life. Hitherto his circle of acquaintances had been drawn exclusively from business contacts but this was beginning to change. Among those who would experience his hospitality at Dambutene were the Dowager Empress of France, Eugénie, widow of Napoleon III, and the Marquis and Marchioness of Breadalbane, well-connected in Liberal circles and the first members of the aristocracy with whom Lipton was to be on friendly terms.

There was curiously in this most conformist of men, Thomas Lipton, a well-buried streak of sympathy for nationalist causes which occasionally surfaced. When in the United States he had expressed the hope that the Land Act would pass in Ireland and now in Ceylon he befriended a man who was certainly not persona grata with the British Government of the day.

This was Arabi Pasha, who had been defeated at Tel-el-Kebir in 1881 by an Egyptian force backed by the British, sentenced to death but then reprieved and permanently exiled to Ceylon. Here Lipton came across him and a mutual liking sprang up to the extent that the Scot awarded the Egyptian a well-paid sinecure with his tea organisation in Ceylon. He went further, and tacitly interested himself in Arabi Pasha's campaign to be allowed to return to Egypt.

Lipton was now a man of some influence and astute enough to use it sparingly. If this irritated the politicians, and it did, the opinions of a man who could write 50,000 cheques to the Exchequer for payment of tea duties alone would certainly receive careful consideration.

If there was a significant watershed in the career of Thomas Lipton then it came in the years 1889-90. Not only was his entry to the tea trade phenomenally successful, and it has to be remembered that this success was in an area of which he knew absolutely nothing until his late forties, but the centre of his business moved south to London and suddenly he was much more than a provincial tradesman made good.

For as long as his parents were alive he had resisted the increasing and rational demand that the headquarters of the whole enterprise should be located in London. The Glasgow warehouse at Lancefield Street was inadequate and because of its cramped surroundings incapable of expansion. More and more the major decisions were being taken in the south and he himself was spending far more nights in sleepers between the two cities than was sensible or good for him. Yet so long as his parents were alive he clung to Glasgow and his Cambuslang home.

In October 1889 his mother died, and in the spring of the following year, his father. It was the classic case: "She, first deceased, he for a little tried To live without her, liked it not and died."

Lipton grieved for his father certainly but the irreparable loss was that of his mother. She had given him the greatest gift in his life, her absolute faith that there were no heights to which Tommy could not ascend. In a very real sense all his achievements had been for her. He had been the most dutiful of sons, indeed it went beyond that since the duty had been a pleasure. As he left the Southern Necropolis on the afternoon of her funeral - it was the very warm out-of-season October day with which Glasgow sometimes climatically teases its inhabitants - he felt literally and metaphorically bereft. It was clear that his father would not survive long nor did he. Now both parents were laid by the side of the four brothers and sisters who had gone before and he was totally alone in the world.

The remedy in such cases is normally for the survivor to work harder. It seemed impossible in Lipton's case but he plunged into new tasks with renewed vigour. He had new challenges to confront. The heart and brains of the operation had to be moved south, premises had to be found in London and he himself would need a house. The one he had in Scotland, Johnstone Villa in Cambuslang, was shut up for a spell before being handed over for use as a nurses' home.

Bath Street, City Road was the location chosen in the heart of London; at least Bath Street would remind him of Glasgow days as it was and is a major thoroughfare in that city. The London version of it would now be the centre for the tea-packing side of things; for the present the manufacture of scones, cakes and shortbread, the Scots being notoriously sweet-toothed, would be left at Lancefield Street in Glasgow.

The re-location of a Scottish industry or commercial concern to England is normally guaranteed to cause a great deal of hostility in the northern kingdom but there was little or nothing of that in this instance. There was wide-spread recognition that Lipton had kept the business in Scotland for as long as was reasonable - perhaps even rather longer - and he left for the south with general and genuine good wishes. The fact that he still came north frequently and was a firm subscriber to Scottish charities also helped. He well knew how to allay prickly Scottish sensibilities, and some years later at the great Glasgow Exhibition of 1901 he endeared himself to his audience by self-deprecatingly beginning his speech "Of course, only the duffers ever leave Glasgow, you know."

The process of removal to London was a major logistical exercise since many of the staff went south too. It was February 1892 before the last batch of 20 office staff, including some half-a-dozen of the new lady "typewriters" as they were initially called, caught the train for London.

It was not until this time when his parents were dead and he had made the move to London that Lipton acquired the first house that could be called exclusively his own.

It was typical of him in that it would be his home for the remainder of his life. The house was Osidge, in the district of Southgate, north of London and just into Hertfordshire. He had stayed briefly at Muswell Hill just before this but Osidge, a low, graceful house with a trellised garden was to be his special pride. He would use it not only to entertain friends and business acquaintances, the latter more than the former, but also every year there was a day of sports and entertainment for the office staff.

Fete to Lipton's employees at Mr. Lipton's residence, Southgate.

He particularly enjoyed such days partly because there was a real kindliness about the man but also because it pleased him greatly to play the patriarch. In the early days after the firm moved to London Osidge was used for its sports days featuring such events as "The Lipton (Tea) Cup - to be run for the human race".

He might be patriarchal but he did not stand on any false dignity. The purchase of a fine house such as Osidge normally brings with it a history of the dwelling, real or imagined. Lipton mentioned that the house had been mentioned in a charter of the monastery of St. Alban's as far back as the reign of King John, under the name Huyeseg. He was not at all put out, indeed laughed heartily when a friend gave his opinion that it was much more likely to be a corruption of the Anglo-Saxon word for sausage.

He developed an interest in the growing of orchids and every day of the working year all managers at headquarters got a flower from the gardens and hothouses at Osidge. Land was bought at White Hart Lane, almost on the site of the Tottenham Hotspur Football Club, for the creation of a sports ground for his employees.

And still the expansion went on. He moved into confectionery and he became a Royal Warrant holder by supplying tea to Queen Victoria; now the outsider had arrived with a vengeance. He was paying cheques to the Exchequer which represented half of an entire week's tea duty for the United Kingdom.

There was little distinction between business and pleasure. By June 1896 the annual outing to Theydon Bois in Essex involved the transporting of more than 2,000 people. This necessitated the hire of 60 four-horse brakes and a procession over a mile in length. Traffic in the east end was stopped as the mighty cortege moved out towards the country at a stately pace. That kind of publicity quite simply could not be bought. His workforce, whether on the stately move towards their day out, or at their daily place of labour, was certainly impressive. In October 1896 his new custom-built premises in City Road were formally opened. Above the main entrance was carved the motto "Work Conquers All". The architects had wanted the Latin version, "Labor Vincit Omnia" but Lipton had rejected this as being pretentious. That did not stop him taking the chance to reveal, as if by accident, that when Her Majesty Queen Victoria took up her summer residence at Balmoral 200pounds of best Lipton tea was sent on ahead of her to Royal Deeside.

The day was fast nearing when he would scarcely have to work to keep his name before the public. The well-doing Glasgow merchant was soon to be moving in social circles so exalted that even his mother, whose faith in him had been boundless, could scarce have credited it.

With 300 clerks in London, 5,000 hands in Ceylon, where already a friend had joked that he owned half the island and had a mortgage on the other half, and with 150 shops throughout Britain of which seven were in his native Glasgow, he did not have time to be daunted.

CHAPTER 5
LIPTON IN SOCIETY

In the spring and early summer of 1897 Britain was engrossed in the preparations for the celebration of Victoria's Diamond Jubilee. The old Queen, far from popular for much of her reign, indeed republicanism was rarely stronger, had by mere dint of survival acquired the status of an icon. She could now have little time to go and the combination of the fast-fading reign and the fast-fading century stirred her subjects into manifestations of loyalty. Troops of potentates would come from all over the Empire and for almost the very last time the kings and queens of Europe would assemble in full panoply.

Sir George Faudel Philipps could therefore be pardoned for congratulating himself on the good fortune of being Lord Mayor of London in such an auspicious year. He was not destined to cherish this illusion for long. Opening *The Times* one morning his attention was drawn to an open letter addressed to himself. Slowly the addressee realised that the signatory was Alexandra, Princess of Wales and Queen in waiting. With a growing sense of utter despair he read the letter.

"In the midst of all the many schemes and preparations for the commemoration of the Queen's Diamond Jubilee when everybody comes forward on behalf of some good cause - when schools, hospitals and other charitable institutions have been so wisely and liberally provided for - there seems to me to be one class that has been overlooked - the poorest of the poor in the slums of London. Might I plead for these - that they should also have some share in the festivities of that blessed day and so remember until the end of their lives that great and good Queen whose glorious reign has by the blessing of God been prolonged for 60 years.

Let us therefore provide these poor beggars and outcasts with a dinner or substantial meal during the week of the 22nd June. I leave it to your very kind and able organisation to arrange that the very poor in all parts of London should be equally cared for".

The princess enclosed with her letter a cheque for £100.

The feelings of the wretched Lord Mayor, Sir George Faudel Philipps are not difficult to imagine. They must have been akin to those of Sir Patrick Spens in the old Scots ballad. Readers will remember that when he too received a royal command transmitted to him by letter the anonymous ballad writer describes his reaction in these graphic words:

"The first word that Sir Patrick read sae loud, sae loud laughed he, The next word that Sir Patrick read, the tear blinded his e'e".

DONOR OF THE ·£25,000.

A NOTEWORTHY CAREER.

IT IS with pleasure we give in our columns this week a short sketch and portrait of T. J. Lipton. Mr Lipton and his parents resided in Cambuslang for a considerable period, occupying a snug little cottage near the railway station; and while the old folks were alive he could be seen on Sunday afternoon mounted on a beautiful charger taking his afternoon ride. Although residing here he took no public interest in local affairs; but when appealed to for subscriptions for any object connected with this district he always responded liberally, and contributes a prize for butter making at the annual show of the Cambuslang, Rutherglen, and Blantyre Agricultural Society, besides supplying tea to the annual treat for old folks of Cambuslang. Mr Lipton has been essentially a thoroughly representative Cambuslang man, and has taken a deep and active part in every movement which had for its object the welfare of the district. Notably, if we mistake not, he contributed liberally towards the building fund of the Cambuslang Institute and also gave a handsome donation towards the erection of the West Established Church, where his father and mother used to worship. Cambuslang has not produced a man who has done more towards the promotion of the village and the welfare of the inhabitants.

The following appreciation of Mr Lipton appeared in the "Weekly Sun," and is from the pen of Mr T. P. O'Connor, M.P., an Irish member, and one of the foremost London journalists.

I don't suppose that Mr Lipton will be a member of the House of Peers; but if sterling character, if the instincts and boundless charity establish claims to such an honour, he certainly would stand a good chance, particularly if he cared for these things. I never had the slightest doubt from the beginning that he was the donor of the princely gift of £25,000 which will enable the fund of the Princess of Wales to be worthily closed. My reason for the supposition was that I knew that Mr Lipton had lunched with the Lord Mayor a day or two before the announcement was made, and for Mr Lipton to go to a lunch is an epoch in his life. I only know of his having done it once before in his busy lifetime, and then it was the house of Lady Jeune—but, then, Lady Jeune has the power of attracting everybody to her hospitable home—for Mr Lipton is almost a recluse. A kind, open-hearted, frank, gregarious man, he, nevertheless, is so absorbed in his business that he regards every moment spent away from it with the same inner regretfulness as the youth who has been separated from his first love. Morning or late, even into the night, you can find Mr Lipton in that inner sanctuary he has in the immense building—or should I call it small town?—from which he rules his kingdom all over the world.

The son of two poor Irish people who found their way to Glasgow some half a century ago—possibly under the stress of that awful famine and fever period which is Ireland's saddest page in this century—Mr Lipton began life under inauspicious stars. When he was a tiny little fellow he was a messenger in a small shop; he slept under the counter, and doubtless, poor lad, he got many a harsh word and many an ugly look. Then he went on board a small coasting vessel, and we all know what kind of life that is. And to-day, still under fifty years of age, he counts his employees by tens of thousands; his business and name are world-wide; and all this he has done by the sheer force of his own will and his indomitable energy and business genius. What that business is in extent may be gathered from one little fact; an offer was made for it of two and a-half millions money; it was refused!

Amid all this success Mr Lipton has remained a modest, retiring, simple man. He is proud of his Irish blood, and loves the Irish cause as heartily as the best Irish patriot. And, finally, here is a little touch about him which will show what a good fellow he is. Above his desk there are three portraits in a single frame. They tell their own tale with a pathos that perhaps an Irishman can best understand. In the centre is the portrait of the erect, slight, wiry, eager-faced man to whom you are talking, and who has a battery of electric bells by his side to summon the heads of the multiform departments that he controls. At either side are two eminently Irish figures; Irish in the simplicity, the antiquity of the dress, in the reverie and gentle melancholy of the faces, in the somewhat compressed lips which suffering and longing and mournful recollections have given to the Irish poor. They are the poor old father and mother of Mr Lipton. Between him and them stretches the black and voiceless sea of death, and the wistful look he often gives up at them tells its own tale of all the inner loneliness there is in the central figure of this bustling and noisy garrison of industry.

MR LIPTON MEETS ROYALTY.

The Prince and Princess of Wales on Saturday last laid the foundation stone of the new Royal Ophthalmic Institution in City Road, adjoining which are Mr Lipton's chief offices and warehouses. The latter were picturesquely decorated in view of the occasion, and on appearing at one of the windows Mr Lipton whose gift of £25,000 to the Princess's Poor Children Fund is the talk of London, received quite an ovation from the assembled crowd. On the arrival of the Royal party the Lord Mayor took the fitting opportunity of presenting Mr Lipton to the Princess, who shook him warmly by the hand and engaged him in lively conversation. At the conclusion of this little function the Lord Mayor and the Mayoress with a distinguished party were conducted over Mr Lipton's immense establishment.

57

The last two sentences of Alexandra's letter are the kernel of it. In a delightfully casual and airy way she left to the Lord Mayor the twin tasks of supervising the actual Fund and of making the logistical arrangements to feed... how many? A hundred thousand? Half a million? And all this to be done inside six weeks and with a cheque which even as a starter was seriously deficient. Nobody, initially anyway, was going to trump the going rate which the royals had established. The Lord Mayor might have been pardoned had he too flirted with republicanism but he did not. He manfully attempted to make the best of an exceedingly bad job.

His beginnings were not propitious. Money was slow to come in, there were other more attractive calls on the public's charity and within the Press considerable opposition to the whole idea which although Alexandra had certainly floated it from a genuine kindliness, was nevertheless seen as condescending and demeaning towards the intended recipients.

The Princess's dinner to the destitute poor: The Great Assembly Hall, Mile End Road.

The Dinner Fund, as the weeks slipped away, showed every sign of being a disaster, and a highly-embarrassing disaster at that, given the direct royal involvement. Lipton in his own story, *Leaves from the Lipton Logs*, was as ever the diplomat when he described the initial reaction to the appeal for funds.

"It was not, to say the least of it, an immediate success. The monied classes of England - always generous to a degree let it be admitted in subscribing to certain types of charities - did not take kindly to the Dinner Fund for some reason or another".

Lipton minimises the difficulty here. Money came in miniscule amounts and at a glacial pace. Three weeks to go and scarce a fifth of the requisite sum was in the hands of the Lord Mayor. The latter was called upon one day by the Scot, who had already pledged himself to supply all the tea and sugar that might be needed. There are two versions of what happened next. On being informed of the poor take-up by Sir George Faudel Philipps, one version has Lipton on the impulse of the moment writing out a cheque for £25,000 and enquiring if this would be enough to safeguard the event.

A more probable version, since it purports to quote from the letter verbatim, is that Lipton wrote the following letter on May 17th when time was indeed fast running out.

"I was exceedingly sorry that subscriptions were coming in so slowly for such a laudable event and I have a strong feeling that this should not be allowed to fall through for lack of support. I have very great pleasure in enclosing a cheque for £25,000". In both versions the donor is said to have expressed a wish that the gift should be anonymous.

Lipton and Philipps were both men of the world and must have known perfectly well that there was absolutely no chance of the donor's identity being kept a secret. The papers amused themselves for a couple of days with a list of possible Samaritans and in an elegant little poem in *The Pelican*, the poet offered a roll-call of contemporary millionaires who might have done the deed, among them the American William Waldorf Astor, the cycle king Mr. Hooley, the South African magnate Barney Barnato and the notorious swindler Horatio Bottomley.

WHO SENT THAT CHEQUE?

Who sent that cheque?
Mr. Astor smiled sadly
"I wish I had, badly
But I didn't send that cheque."

Who sent that cheque?
Barney wired "Please mention
I'd no such intention.
I didn't send that cheque".

Who sent that cheque?
Mr. Hooley was pleasant
"Oh no, not my present.
I didn't send that cheque".

Who sent that cheque?
Mr. Bottomley said "Sonny,
Hansard folks have my money.
I didn't send that cheque".

Who sent that cheque?
Mr. Lowenfeld said "Nein,
The glory's not mine.
I didn't send that cheque".

Neither Philipps or Lipton was a child in the big world. Payment by cheque meant detection was swift and certain and no doubt was meant to be so. The faintly unsavoury aspect of the business was the announcement that a bank cashier had made an unauthorised disclosure. An American newspaper, and that was an area almost invariably friendly to Lipton, rather waspishly congratulated him on keeping such an important secret inviolate for an entire afternoon. The *Bristol Times* of June 25 1897 was much kinder. "Thanks to Thomas Lipton the Jubilee dinner to the London poor was a comparative success. But for his interest the scheme would have been a fiasco as the Royals themselves contributed practically nothing".

What were Lipton's motives in all this? Mixed, almost certainly. It would be quite wrong to deny him any feelings at all of philanthropy in the venture; he was and it cannot be over-emphasised, a genuinely kindly man. At the same time he had to know that Alexandra and more importantly her husband, the Prince of Wales would be very likely to be grateful to the man who had rescued the Princess from the humiliation of a failed appeal.

The future Edward VII's heart was engaged elsewhere, chiefly with Mrs. Alice Keppel, but he was always fond of his impulsive wife and would be glad that she had been extricated from a potentially damaging situation. The following Christmas Lipton received a handsome diamond scarf pin from the grateful Alexandra and small paragraphs began to appear in the Press suggesting that in the near future plain Thomas might become Sir Thomas. These fliers were always followed by others explaining that this would not happen in the next Honours List as that was not the way the British system worked, perish the thought. This proved correct, his name was missing from the Jubilee List but was there at New Year 1898 and on a duty meeting to convey his thanks to Lipton, Edward, Prince of Wales, discovered that he got on with this merchant very well indeed.

The future Edward VII was a complex man. He has been represented as bluff, hail-fellow-well-met, almost democratic. This, given the mores of his time, is ludicrous. What he was was someone much more receptive to the world than Victoria could be, a man who admired those other men who had been fortunate enough to carve their destinies from an early age. His own life had been spent in waiting, interminable waiting; by this stage he was 57 years of age and still at some distance from the throne. Barred from any contact with affairs of state by his mother from motives of mistrust and perhaps jealousy, he not surprisingly turned to frivolous habits and dissipated companions. Long before this he had been cited in a divorce action and given testimony in a gambling case.

He could be a formidably snobbish figure to those who crossed him, although his bile was chiefly reserved for those who might be described as semi-permanently at court. On one occasion when a guest at Windsor had the temerity to appear in tweeds for the drive to Ascot, Edward made a point of stopping next to him and enquiring in a loud voice "Goin' rattin' Harris?"

He was kinder with those who, like Lipton, did not pose any social threat. It should be remembered that the Prince was at odds with several of the largest and most conservative noble families who considered their own lineage to be demonstrably superior to that of the Hanoverians and that the Marlborough House set, as the prince's friends were called, were thoroughly disreputable.

Lipton was different. He was properly deferential to the Prince but never servile. He could tell jokes and stories which genuinely made the Prince laugh but rarely if ever transgressed the bounds of subject and monarch. He was rich, and therefore sought nothing tangible from the future King. Later they would discover a common interest in yachting and the King would find that Lipton was a useful sounding-board in his own attempts to come to an understanding of the other great English-speaking country, the United States of America.

Such a relationship would of course always be on the terms of the prince-king but it was sufficiently well-grounded to survive until Edward's death in 1910. It was certainly on a nudge from Edward, possibly prompted by Alexandra, that Thomas Lipton in January 1898 became one of the few Britons to cross the sea to be knighted. He did this because the venue for his investiture was Osborne, on the Isle of Wight, where the aged Queen spent her last years and where she would die a couple of years later.

Lipton must have marvelled at the upturns and downturns in human fortunes as he first stood and then knelt in the presence of this tiny figure who was Empress of India. Did he remark on the unexpectedly foreign voice as she dubbed him knight? Did he wonder what his mother would have made of it, that the little boy from Crown Street, her youngest, Tommy, was in the presence of a woman who ruled almost half the known world at that moment?

5. LIPTON'S "LEADING LINE" is one of which he may feel justly proud. It will be gratefully discussed by thousands of London's poor on the event of the Princess of Wales's dinner to the destitute.

We do not know because Lipton does not mention it, showing an unwonted reticence about one of the greatest honours conferred upon him in a lifetime of honours. He may have felt that he had bought his knighthood, and in a sense he may well have done, but the record of solid achievement was there. His honour was well-received by Press and people and as a West Country paper growled in response to an isolated, snobbish protest "Better to knight a merchant of tea than a butcher of natives" a cutting reference to several major-generals who were being knighted for extending the British Empire and the Pax Britannica by means of the employment of the Gatling and Maxim against native tribes who were less well equipped.

In the matter of the Jubilee Dinner he had no need to reproach himself either. He had not only written the cheque; that was comparatively unimportant, any one of a dozen millionaires could have done that. What was much more vital was that he had taken complete charge of the catering arrangements on the day. Only a consummate professional could have carried through a scheme for tens of thousands of people to be fed and watered in nine widely separate areas of London. He was the ideal man to do it too for these were the kind of people on whom his original little shops had been built. A tenet of his creed was "to be civil to rich and poor alike" and he discharged this self-imposed obligation with a natural courtesy.

At the same time he cemented the affections of the city wherein he had been born. Shortly after his knighthood had been conferred he gave a general newspaper interview in which he said "My prime ambition is always to be regarded as a Glasgow man". The thing he ought to have said perhaps, but there is ample evidence that he meant it, his will would prove it, and certainly no remaining honour in a life which had still over thirty years to run would mean as much to him as the bestowal upon him of the Freedom of Glasgow in 1923.

Opposite. Sir T. J. Lipton in the uniform of a Lieutenant of the City of London.

CHAPTER 6
A SOLITARY MAN

As the nineteenth century shaded into the present one Sir Thomas Lipton was one of Victoria's wealthiest subjects and he was unmarried. His wealth alone would have ensured his eligibility but when one added to that his tall, good-looking presence and his almost invariable affability, it is small wonder that press and public were not disposed to rest content until they had triumphantly married him off.

In this they had misread their man. Lipton would from time to time remind his listeners that since the death of his parents he was completely alone in the world, but he showed absolutely no sign of wanting to do anything to alleviate that situation. The newspapers might cajole, hint and even occasionally assert but he was not to be stampeded into matrimony by them or anyone else.

Not surprisingly therefore, what newspapers and biographers could not establish they cast around to make up. Even in Alec Waugh's otherwise perceptive biography, *The Lipton Story*, there is a derisory chapter in which the writer purports to tell the great love story of Lipton's life. The vigilant reader will be on his guard from the first sentence of the relevant chapter which begins with the assertion that in 1885 Catherine McLeod was living in a small village between Gorrock (sic) and Ashton on the northeast coast of Scotland. If this were so then it must, with Brigadoon, have confined itself to appearing once every hundred years, since no study of a map reveals it. Gourock and Ashton are of course on the Clyde coast just on the seaward side of Greenock but north-east they are not.

In this sad lapse from his normal high standards Waugh tells us tremulously of the young girl being greatly taken by the handsome middle-aged businessman, driving around in his horse and trap. He greatly impresses the girl with talk of his early travels but after a stay of six weeks in this village he disappears as suddenly as he had come, leaving Catherine with but an inscribed photograph of himself, which she kept ever afterwards. The chronology is at a glance impossible. At this stage Lipton was still totally involved in building up the largest retail grocery chain in Britain. The whole enterprise so depended on his personal supervision, that he could not take a week's holiday, let alone six.

From the newspapers' point of view this was quite unsatisfactory. Here you had a well-respected figure on both sides of the Atlantic and his wedding would be most noteworthy; as the British film of the 1930s said, "This Man Is News". The journalistic adage of not allowing the facts to spoil a good story was exemplified to the full. In August 1898 the *Inter Ocean* of Chicago excitedly reported that Sir Thomas was engaged to marry one of the daughters of Sir George Faudel

Opposite. Sir Thomas Lipton at his London office in 1897. Not yet fifty he was already a multi-millionaire employing thousands of people.

Philipps but it did not distinguish between the Lord Mayor's two girls, Stella and Nellie.

Perhaps the signs could have been better read had men noticed the two qualities for which the ladies praised him. Time and again they mention that the most striking of his characteristics are his good nature and quintessential boyishness. Throughout his life he very largely retained the capacity to be surprised and delighted but was there, where women were concerned, a certain lack of gravitas?

Certainly, in the harmless Victorian fashion he was a ladies man and adept flirt. He positively enjoyed the company of women but his preference was strongly for them in the plural. On one occasion he was asked to choose the most beautiful chorus-girl in New York from a short-list which had thoughtfully been narrowed down to two. Confronted with these two "broilers" as chorus girls of 18 and under were then quaintly known, Lipton deliberated solemnly and protractedly before stating that he was quite unable to give any decision since they were both totally exquisite.

It has to be remembered that the Press on either side of the Atlantic was then far less inquisitive and prurient than it would be today. There was great interest in Lipton's matrimonial prospects, yes, but it was essentially a friendly curiosity. On a visit to his steamyacht, the *Erin*, one of several made by her, the young Rose Fitzgerald was jocularly proposed to by Sir Thomas and as jocularly accepted. Both knew pefectly well that Rose would marry Joseph Kennedy and were happy to leave it at that.

The supposed alliance with the daughter of a wealthy Chicago family, Alice Revell, seemed more possible, and since Lipton was out of the country at the time this evoked a rather embarrassed denial from the girl herself. There was a sense in which the United States had gone oddly mad over "Jubilee" Lipton, not that he was averse to keeping that particular flame well stoked. It is ironical that his most serious contretemps over the marital status should have come in an area in which he was outstandingly good, namely press relations.

Even with his abundant good will, it was clear that from time to time he would be too pressed by business concerns to accommodate all requests for interview. This landed him in trouble in Chicago in July 1898 when he asked a local reporter to wait for an interview until that evening. The chagrined reporter, although the request had been made with all courtesy, then did what reporters have done since the beginning of time and simply invented a conversation the two were supposed to have had.

Opposite. Sir Thomas entertains the three daughters of the ex-Mayor of Boston, Mrs Joseph Kennedy, Miss Eunice and Miss Agnes Fitzgerald on his steam yacht Victoria. 24th July 1920.

In this piece the reporter declared that Sir Thomas had stated that he was tired of the solitary life. "The time has come for me to take unto myself a wife, and I have a long-standing preference for American ladies." The predictable outcome was that within an hour of the newspaper hitting the streets, the hotel where Lipton was staying was beset with anxious, determined women, scanning the various exits from the hotel with gimlet eye. Young, mature, pretty, plain, well-doing, poor, they sat there with such assiduity that Lipton was confined to his suite.

He did his best to laugh it off, protesting to the man from the *Chicago Tribune* that "it was a mean advantage to take of an unprotected fellow" but there was a real anger there and in private he complained bitterly of this outrageous treatment of a visitor to the United States. Gradually he learned that any pronouncement on the subject, however light-heartedly intended, could rebound on him.

An instance of this was his speech at the Hotel Cecil in London in November 1901 after his return from New York and his second unsuccessful attempt at the Blue Riband of yachting, the America's Cup, He said:- "I have been asked if we two bachelors, Mr. Watson (the defeated Yacht's designer) and I would get married if we won the Cup. Well, I cannot speak for Mr. Watson but for myself is one big job at a time not enough?"

Gradually the rumours dwindled in both frequency and intensity and there was a somewhat wondering acceptance of the fact that Sir Thomas was and would remain a bachelor. There was a brief flurry when he received his baronetcy in 1901. This was an hereditary title and the feeling was that the honour might kindle dynastic ambitions but he gave absolutely no sign of this and so the dignity came and went with him.

Let us try to answer the incessant question of the newspapers, why? The first thing to do is to refrain from back-projecting our contemporary notions of morality to the last century. Today a prominent man who opts to remain single will have serious questions asked about his sexual orientation, unless he is a noted rake. Libertine or homosexual is the dismal choice of tags that await him. It can safely be said that Lipton was neither.

In the same way that he could move across social classes with a complete surefootedness, so he could be a squire of dames or a man's man and be equally convincing in either role. His chances of being a roué were in any case severely limited by the fact that he lived under his parents' roof until he was forty and for most of this time his work-rate was manic. Then again, although never an assiduous church-goer, he was strongly influenced by the dutiful, almost ascetic, life that his parents had led.

Opposite. On board Erin, June 1906. Although a confirmed bachelor there was no shortage of female company on his cruises.

To be a bachelor in the nineteenth century was not at all rare. Kitchener was a bachelor, so too was Arthur Balfour.

The affectionate regard of the bachelor was strongly reinforced in fiction through such characters as Sherlock Holmes, the Cheeryble Brothers of Dickens, and G.B. Shaw's Professor Higgins and Colonel Pickering. Remember also Lipton's abiding axiom:- "Work is more fun than fun". Since he was 10 years old his energies had been entirely engaged by work. He ate it, drank it, dreamt it. It may well have been that he felt it unfair to confront any wife with such a powerful rival, to subject her to a contest in which the result was foredoomed.

Waugh coins one very memorable phrase, dealing with Lipton as the driven man. He says:- "Perhaps chastity was his short-cut". Lipton was ready with words, quick to frame the clever phrase which would take the questioning to a safer area. Thus, when asked "Why have you never married, Sir Thomas?" his stock answer always was "I have never met any lady who measured up to my mother".

He may very well have been telling them the literal truth.

Beauties on the Lipton yacht. Lady John Ferguson and Miss Nan Jarvis watch the races.

By 1898 Lipton had finally yielded to the public clamour - in his own time and on his own terms - and to allow his enterprise to become a limited company.

There would never be a better time for it. His knighthood had placed him favourably in the public eye, as had his philanthropic saving of the jubilee dinner, and the knowledge that he would shortly challenge for the America's Cup gave him something of the status of the national champion. In a sense it was an inevitable step. Even such an impressive business as his was not proof against buy-out offers and he had already rejected a bid of £2 million from the tyre king E.T. Hooley.

The City was inclined to look rather sniffily on the plethora of enthusiastic newspaper articles which accompanied the news of the launch. The stock market magazine, the *Statist,* on March 5th 1898 wrote in a style of grave rebuke: "It is well to bear in mind that boomed issues have often shown a speedy reaction from an undue market hoist".

The plan as set out in the prospectus called for capital of £1 million in Cumulative Preference Shares, £1 million in Ordinary shares of £1 for which a five shilling premium would be required on each share purchased and £500,000 of Debenture Stock to be redeemed after September 1920 at 115%. It is interesting that the City did not regard this as a particularly exciting or attractive issue, bearing in mind that it was competing with such rivals for the investor's purse as the vibrant South African minerals market and a flurry of similar activity in the Yukon and the western states of the United States.

The Lipton business was seen as rock-solid, but perhaps no longer capable of drastic expansion; slow steady growth would be its watchward. Not a bad investment by any means, but not one to stir the blood. But that was the professional and informed viewpoint and it overlooked the magic of the Lipton name for the layman. If Lipton was recommending this, then no other endorsement was needed.

The share issue was to cause the kind of frenetic excitement that occurs only rarely. Indeed comparisons were made with the rush to invest in the Darien Company in Scotland in the 1690s and the South Sea Bubble of the early eighteenth century. The required capital was over-subscribed twenty-fold and investors pleaded with the Scottish magnate to take their money. In the firm's counting-house extra staff had to be taken on to deal with the tidal wave of applications, and Lipton with that sureness of touch which almost never deserted him, saw to it that the suspense was heightened and protracted by arranging to send out the notices of refusal first.

CHAPTER 7
LIPTON BECOMES A LIMITED COMPANY

Always one to give a good story legs he made himself freely available to pressmen to tell them something of the incredible public response. In those more docile days for the Fourth Estate, the man from the *Daily Mail* obligingly fed him a donkey-drop question: "You have been making a lot of nice new friends lately, Sir Thomas. You have been astonished I dare say, to find how many know of you of whom you have never heard?"

Lipton's reply could have been penned by W.S. Gilbert "I received a letter with an application for shares from a gentleman who said that nine years ago he was a passenger on a P. & O. boat in the East and he endeavoured to recall himself to my memory by the circumstance that he once passed me the mustard".

The general opinion in the city was that Lipton had pulled off a master stroke. He, the vendor, would be getting much more than any businessman would consider to be the full value of all the assets of the business, including the good will, and he would have the shares and debentures besides. In effect he got £2 million for the sale and he still retained a very large shareholding.

Consistent throughout his life was his abhorrence of the middleman. In any form of business activities he had avoided using the services of any firm of brokers. He was not so arrogant as to believe, however, that he could carry off such a gigantic financial transaction entirely on his own while continuing to run the day to day business of the firm.

His mentor and aide-de-camp in the company flotation was, on the surface, a strange choice. Panmure Gordon's Caledonian name may well have commended him to Lipton. He was an odd mixture of extravagance in his own personal life - he was the owner of literally hundreds of suits, hats and pairs of boots - and unremitting prudence in the conduct of the affairs of others. It was his idea to charge a five shilling premium on every pound share and by doing this he guaranteed that he would put a quarter of a million pounds in Lipton's pocket. He appears to have done at least that, for Lipton was to say subsequently that the entire cost of Shamrock II and the expense of his second challenge for the America's Cup were defrayed from the profits on the sale estimated at well over £300,000.

He was at the very apex of his commercial success and yet it is from this point that matters very slowly begin to go slightly awry. He might still be the presiding genius of the company but perhaps he could accept more readily with the head than with the heart the fact that there was a sense in which it would never again be entirely his business. There was now a new element, accountability to the other shareholders and these, timid at first in the presence of the great man, would increasingly want to know more details not only of company profits, but of its long-term strategy.

Top. The rush for Lipton shares at the National Bank of Scotland.

Bottom. Lipton with his private secretaries in his London office.

There was another aspect. Lipton found, possibly to his own surprise, that he was not naturally gifted at making these explanations and accountings. He, who rightly prided himself on being able to comport himself admirably with all manner of people and in all manner of circumstance, found that he could not do this at all readily in the new business context. When he took questions from the floor when chairing his first Annual General Meeting he sounded strangely vague and then surprisingly tetchy.

This was understandable of course. For thirty years he had effectively been an Executive Committee of one. He knew exactly what he was doing, the results were there for all to see. Why should he now be shackled by the need to report minutely to people who had no idea of the intricacies of his trade? The answer was simple, he had taken the money and from now on this was the way things had to be.

There was yet another ball in play. He had made this major change at exactly the time when his own life style was changing. Hitherto he had been truly impervious to the lure of the social scene. In his first twenty years in London he claimed to have been in the theatre only once and to have fallen asleep during the performance. There is no reason to disbelieve him, it squares with everything we know about him hitherto.

Suddenly in the late 1890s his name begins to appear with increasing frequency in the Social and Personal columns. He attends dinners, he appears on the guest list at society weddings. He finds that he is an accomplished after-dinner speaker. He appears on the fringes of royal occasions and it is noted that he now spends part of the winter in Cairo or on the French Riviera. This mattered not a jot of course when he had himself to please. The irony is that when he had only himself to consider he did not do these things but now the pattern would be one of increasingly alert scrutiny from his fellow shareholders. Eventually, after the end of the First World War although the involvement in the America's Cup could be argued to be the best advertisement the company ever had, there would be those to argue that "The Old Man" spent too much time aboard the *Shamrock* and too little in his offices in City Road.

His yachting exploits will be dealt with at some length and separately because they helped rather than hindered the business, and they especially contributed to what was probably Lipton's finest achievement, the cementing of good relations with the United States at the time of an uneasy rivalry between the two great countries.

By July 1898 when Lipton had been besieged by the many American ladies who liked the notion of being Lady Lipton, he was very well-known at least on the eastern sea-board where any news of "Jubilee Lipton" as he was now called were eagerly seized upon. This does not mean that he could count upon universal recognition; the *California Herald* was a little wide of the mark with a well-meant and laudatory article on James J. Tipton.

Certainly the outside world was prepared to place major and difficult commissions in his hands. In January of that year at the height of the Klondyke gold rush he had been asked to provide Dawson City with 500 tons of pork. This cargo was conveyed by special train from Chicago to San Francisco and thence by boat to Alaska.

Occasionally his enthusiasm for America and things American led him to overstep the bounds of prudence or even good sense.

In 1898 during the Spanish-American War, at his new business headquarters in Hoboken, across the river from Manhattan, he unfurled a huge Stars and Stripes from an equally enormous flagstaff with the following stirring speech: "This flag of freedom now unfurled must never be lowered until the Stars and Stripes floats over every government building in Havana and until every Spanish soldier is driven from Cuba. God bless the flag and three cheers for Old Glory".

These utterances so pleased the Daughters of the American Revolution that when he was returning to England he was presented with a Stars and Stripes, seven feet by five feet, made of pure silk with a gilded eagle at the top of the pole. Lipton further endeared himself to the ladies by waving this flag vigorously as the ship slid from the pier out into the main channel.

As he waved his flag in a slow swirling last farewell to the Manhattan piers, he knew exactly what he had to do to ensure that never again would he be James J. Tipton in the vast republic. He, the Glasgow boy made good, would do something which the aristocracy of Great Britain would envy, something they themselves had spent a half-century in vainly attempting. He would turn yachtsman and regain the America's Cup which had remained in American hands since the inception of the races for it in 1851.

The mention of the name of Sir Thomas Lipton today is almost as likely to draw a remark about his repeated challenges to United States yachting supremacy as any comment on his business abilities and achievements. In his quixotic sporting duels with the United States he took on the role and appearance of national champion.

In truth, apart from the financial aspect he was not particularly well-equipped to do so. The Crown Street Yacht Club could at best have been a youthful enthusiasm and although he was to say that when he had a few fugitive hours of leisure as a young man he liked nothing better than to take a sail-boat out on the Clyde these instances could not have been very numerous. To do this he would have needed to go as far down river as Gourock on the south bank or Helensburgh on the north bank. Such a jaunt would have used up a whole day and we have his abundant testimony elsewhere that he hardly every allowed himself such a luxury.

Thomas Lipton very seldom acted on pure impulse although he often liked to give the impression of so doing. He chose yachting because it was the best way of pleasing the king and of keeping his name before the British and above all the American public. Had he lived one hundred years later he might well have sponsored an association football side but that was not a sport which engaged both countries. This was equally true of baseball and as yet golf was not sufficiently broad-based. It is true that yachting then as now was the preserve of the rich but there was a genuine maritime rivalry to be exploited, indeed some sources would have it that Lipton was directed to the possibilities of the America's Cup by the king himself.

The celebrated English author George Orwell has declared that there is nothing like international sport to guarantee ill-will among nations and certainly the history of the America's Cup has been one of recrimination and litigation since its inception. It had all started harmlessly enough back in 1851 when the *America* came across the Atlantic to challenge thc best that British yachtsmen could produce.

The Royal Yacht Squadron at Cowes was the equivalent of the Royal and Ancient Golf Club of St. Andrews and the Marylebone Cricket Club. It was totally socially exclusive and its fiat was law on racing matters at sea. It evinced no great haste to accept the *America's* challenge and eventually the Yankee visitor had to pit her qualities not against a nominated British boat but against all comers in a challenge race for a silver cup. Unusually for top-class races there was no time allowance and no rules as to maximum or minimum size of the competing yachts.

Opposite. Sir Thomas J. Lipton, 1901. A successful businessman and very eligible bachelor.

Above. Shamrock II.

Below. Shamrock III.

Opposite. Shamrock I.

America won by an embarrassing 24 minutes margin so pronounced that when Queen Victoria enquired as to the identity of the yacht in second place one of her naval officers offered the opinion "Your Majesty, there is no second". The cup went back to the United States on the *America*, was handed over by its captain, Commodore Stevens, to the New York Yacht Club and seemed likely to remain there in perpetuity.

This was not from want of effort to recapture it. There were six attempts between 1868-95 which had in common a complete lack of success. The last challenge, that of the Earl of Dunraven, had not only been a losing one but had sparked off an international incident. The America's Cup has always been a peculiarly litigious event and grounds of complaint were never hard to find. Dunraven probably had right on his side when he complained that the throngs of excursion boats crammed with spectators had fatally obstructed the course and it was clearly the responsibility of the defending club, the New York Yacht Club, to see that there was a clear fairway. Furthermore, the American *Defender* and the British *Valkyrie* collided so that the *Valkyrie's* top shrouds were carried away. Both ships sailed on and the *Valkyrie* crossed the line first but the win was annulled as the race committee held the *Valkyrie's* captain at fault for the collision.

By this time Dunraven was convinced that he had no chance of obtaining simple justice in this sporting event. Its most disfiguring element, the circumvention of rules of construction and limitations on canvas spread and size, seemed to him blatant, and growing ever more exasperated he simply came to the starting line for the next race and immediately retired, in effect giving *Defender* a walk-over.

This was bad enough but on his return to England Dunraven went into print in *The Field* with the accusation that before a race the American yacht had been given extra ballast to make her sail lower in the water and therefore faster, and that this extra ballast was clandestinely taken away after the race. This was a slur on the honour of the New York Yacht Club and it had to be rebutted. A court of enquiry was convened and Dunraven attended in person, a prominent English barrister G.K. Askwith in tow. The committee ruled against him.

Set in cold print it looks rather petty but tempers at the time were extremely frayed. Dunraven himself is interesting on the matter:- "When I went over to attend a very belated enquiry I was smuggled out of the liner at Sandy Hook. My good friend Maitland Kersey took lodgings for me close to the New York Yacht Club and I was under close police protection. A protest has nothing to do with motives or responsibilities. It is a mere question of facts - whether so-and-so happened or did not happen, whether this or that was done or not done, whether the protest was frivolous or justified; but when the facts became submerged in a great wave of emotion they are lost sight of and a protest became absurd. I don't say whether evidence was or was not withheld, but I am very sure that not one of the American crew of the tender in which we lived would have dared to give evidence against the *Defender* had they wished to do so. Well, I am not going to reopen that question even to myself. But I thought at the time, and I think still that to raise a game or a race to such a pitch is not conducive to real sport".

Dunraven might well have been an over-pedantic man, there is something of it in the style of the writing, but he found an ally in the magazine *Truth*. "Not a year goes by without some trouble being threatened in almost every branch of sport. For the sake of peace and quietness such events as races for the America's Cup are rather to be deprecated than otherwise".

Quite true, so far as it went, but this was to overlook the genuine maritime rivalry between the two great English speaking nations which had not always been recreational. Sea-faring men on both sides of the Atlantic could recall the exploits of John Paul Jones and Barry in the War of Independence and the great duel of the *Shannon* and the *Chesapeake* in the later war of 1812. The solution was not to stifle the rivalry but to steer it into healthier channels.

Nevertheless, the fact that it was Lipton who picked up the gage left on the ground by the Americans was surprising to most people, and especially surprising, and not particularly pleasing, to the Royal Yacht Squadron. There was nothing in the terms of the race which said that any British challenge had to emanate from the Royal Yacht Squadron but that had always been the tacit assumption and now someone was challenging who was not a member of that august institution. Lipton would sail under the colours of the Royal Ulster Yacht Club and, given his antecedents, this would no doubt be a more meaningful provenance for him.

The challenge was issued in 1898 with the races to be sailed the following summer and immediately the establishment at Cowes in the Isle of Wight, where the Royal Yacht Squadron was located, let their mingled exasperation and amusement be known. A local newspaper ghosted an article which began "Yacht racing is one of the more recognisable ways of losing a fortune. Here at Cowes there is a mingled surprise and mirth that a person should challenge for the America's Cup who hardly knows the stern of a boat from the bow".

Of all the misconceptions of Georgian and Victorian life few are as wide of the mark as the notion that sport was somehow or other a democratising influence. Henley was barred to tradesmen until well into this century, golf clubs vied with each other in their exclusivity. Professional cricketers and footballers had no social standing whatsoever and it was social death for a gentleman to play either game for pay.

The opposition to Lipton was therefore largely based on genuine snobbery; it was the Kaiser who complained that his uncle Edward, when king, was "off boating with his grocer" but there were many Englishmen who thought this without having the courage to say so. There was also the dread thought that perhaps this parvenu could do something which they had been unable to do and bring the "old mug" back across the Atlantic.

Lipton wished to win for his country and the king, but that could not be at the expense of his business prospects. So what should he call his yacht? He decided against any English title straight away. Any name such as *Windsor* or *St. George* would give the impression of that effortless superiority which so annoyed Americans. Nor was a Scots name a starter, the Scots being comparatively unimportant in the United States, having been much more prone to settle in Canada or Australia.

The Irish connection was a different matter. There was an immense Irish colony in the States by this time, growing in wealth and influence. They would be glad to see Britain discomfited but increasingly they came to want Lipton to win because of his personal qualities. They could therefore support Lipton in the safe knowledge that if a yacht called *Shamrock* were to win, it could be represented as a triumph for that "most distressful country".

Above all, Lipton saw the races as a chance to mend fences. There were still those in Britain who felt that Dunraven had received less than fair play. A London clubman's magazine, the *St. James Budget*, commented in August 1898 "If the Americans will kindly take up their submarine contact mines and not arrange a torpedo display on the day of the race there is no reason why an English yacht should not get fair play. The New York Yacht Club must realise that acceptance of the challenge involves responsibility for keeping the course absolutely clear".

To some extent Lipton was compromising right from the outset. He had hoped to challenge with an Irish-built yacht, probably from Harland and Wolff of Belfast, with an Irish crew, skipper, and name, and under the flag of the Royal Ulster Yacht Club.

However, there could be a hard side to Lipton, and one of his more chilling maxims was "Never deal with an unsuccessful man". This, to his mind, was a reason for bypassing the most celebrated yacht designers of the day, George L. Watson, and Beavor Webb, who had been associated with previous America's Cup failures. This proved slightly awkward when later Lipton had to fall back on Watson to design another *Shamrock*. For the moment his choice as designer fell on Wm. Fife Junior of the famous boat-building firm of Fife's of Fairlie, a village near Largs on the Ayrshire coast.

In the end the building of the yacht *Shamrock I* was a rather scattered affair with Thorneycroft of Chiswick making the metal parts of the vessel before she was masted and sparred at Harland and Wolff. This was a kind of consolation prize for the Irish firm after Lipton had realised that they lacked the necessary expertise to carry the whole project through. There was a certain amount of Scottish chagrin that the yacht had not been built on the Clyde, the river that had so to speak given him his start, but all were agreed that the final product was formidable. The estimated price for her construction had been £100,000 but by the time she took to the water she had cost an additional £40,000. At around the same time Lipton had bought himself a steam yacht, the *Nahma* which had been built at Clydebank for the American millionaire Robert Goelet, paying £80,000 for it.

Even this was not what he had in mind to take over to New York for the races and another foreigner, Count Ignacio Florio of Palermo provided him with his new boat, the *Aegusa*, which he set about re-christening. Obviously the new name had to be Irish and he flirted with *Killarney* and *Erin's Isle* before settling on the plainer *Erin*. Then it was time to cross the Atlantic and put his work to the test.

The Erin.

The rules of the America's Cup were very firmly written in favour of the defender. The chief disadvantage which the challenger suffered was that his boat must be capable of making the Trans-Atlantic voyage "on her own bottom". This meant of course a sturdiness of build which the defender need not have since it was only going to be asked to race just offshore and indeed, would not have to do that if the weather was any way

The Dewey Naval Parade.

severe. Even some Americans, annoyed at the discrepancy in requirements, described the coming races as a contest between a bluff ketch, the British entry, and a glorified skimming dish, the American boat.

Before a sail had been hoisted Lipton had brought off a marvellous publicity coup. Early one morning, while he was on the *Erin*, he realised that a United States warship which had hove in sight must be the U.S.S. *Olympia*, the flagship of Admiral Dewey, arriving a little before she was expected, from the battle of Manila Bay in The Spanish War.

All his life Lipton had known a great opportunity when he saw one and he now suddenly realised that the great Admiral had arrived back in triumph from Manila and that no one else knew as yet. It was the work of a second to order the *Erin's* launch to be prepared and have it steer for the *Olympia* so that Lipton could present his compliments to the returned hero. He and Dewey in fact breakfasted together, and later on the Admiral would return the call by coming over to the *Erin*.

Dewey would already have known of Lipton because when the *Olympia* had called in at Ceylon he had sent a quantity of tea to its crew as a gift. Lipton was firmly established in his character of wealthy and amiable bachelor who was a plain good fellow and whose love for the United States was patently genuine.

There was the occasional muttering in the American press that perhaps Admiral Dewey should have taken care to report to his commander-in-chief, the President, before granting any other interviews, but there was also a general acceptance that this was the kind of thing that Lipton did and, as on many other occasions, his essential good nature was the saving of him.

He was given the singular honour of being allowed to lead the port column of the yachting division of the grand water parade which formally marked the return of Admiral Dewey to New York. The *Bristol Mercury* commented slyly on September 29th 1899 "It is difficult to tell whether the festivities at New York are meant for Admiral Dewey or for Sir Thomas Lipton". He had also somehow managed to get himself on the saluting base in Madison Square Garden.

Two days later he was at the Waldorf Astoria for a dinner given to the "jackies" as the ratings and petty officer equivalent of the United States Navy were called. Lipton was greatly intrigued by this situation, knowing that it could have had no parallel in the more rigidly class-structured Britain. It was difficult to imagine a couple of ships' companies taking over Claridge's or the Savoy. He was prevailed upon to make a speech, not that he needed over-persuading. In the course of his address he said:- "I am delighted to get this opportunity to meet you all. The country is proud of you and has welcomed you royally. ... I mean to try to get a little American property here myself and I hope that when that little engagement comes off you won't squash it up like you did the Spanish fleet at Manila."

In home waters *Shamrock* had comfortably seen off the royal yacht *Britannia*, the fastest opposition to be found to put against her but the America's Cup itself was a different matter. The defender, *Columbia* had been designed by the great American boatbuilder Nathaniel Herreshoff and was altogether too powerful for a comparatively inexperienced captain and crew. It should be remembered that Lipton himself had no real experience of racing at this level. The contest was not even close.

This was not to say that the effort had been in vain although there were those in the British camp after the first challenge of 1899 who would say that the United States could always find more millionaires and therefore command more technical expertise than any British challenger ever could. Lipton was far from downcast, he had made the usual optimistic noises before racing started, but in truth he had scarcely expected to be successful first time out. Even if this had not been his primary intention, the races had been a wonderful advertisement for his enterprises.

And it was not too fanciful to say that he had rendered his country service in another sphere. The Boer War was getting under way and there was considerable anti-British feeling in the United States at the spectacle, as it appeared to Americans, of Mother England once more throwing her weight about against a handful of hapless colonists. In fact the Boer War and the Spanish-American War were equally reprehensible but one was "our" war and the other was not, as Americans saw it.

Had Germany actively intervened in this debate in America, there would have been great opportunity for mischief-making but Lipton's support for the United States against Spain was gratefully remembered and helped to temper anti-British sentiment. He left in good spirits. The cream of American society had visited his palatial quarters on the steam yacht *Erin*. He had indicated his intention to challenge again and he would have experience to draw on. Above all, the contest had been conducted in a good spirit and friendly messages had passed between President McKinley and the Prince of Wales. Lipton valued his friendship with the heir to the throne greatly and this consideration probably outweighed all others. The races may have been one-sided, the *Columbia* winning three in succession, but at least the ghost of Lord Dunraven had been laid for the time.

THE DISASTER TO "SHAMROCK II" OFF THE WIGHT: THE KING'S NARROW ESCAPE.

Above. Sir Thomas Lipton at the launch of Shamrock II on the Clyde, 20th April 1901.

Below. Mrs. George Keppel, Mrs. John Drexel, and Mrs. Jameson on the S.Y. Erin.

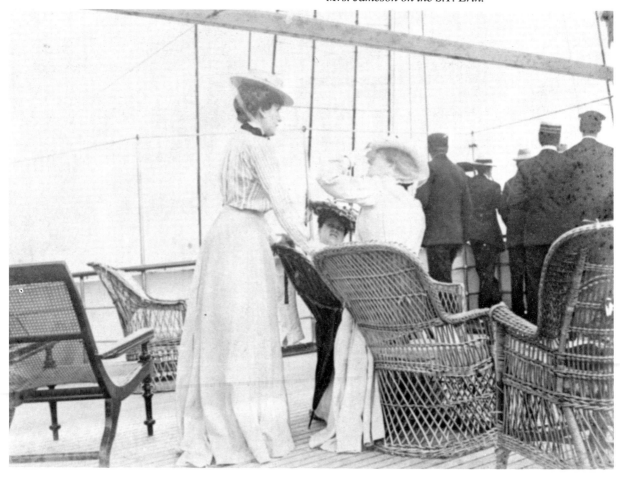

Edward, Prince of Wales was pleased. His purgatory of waiting was now almost at an end, and he was formulating his own ideas on foreign policy. He would not, as a constitutional monarch, be able to run counter to the will of his Cabinet, but he might well be able to influence and he was anxious for good relations with the United States.

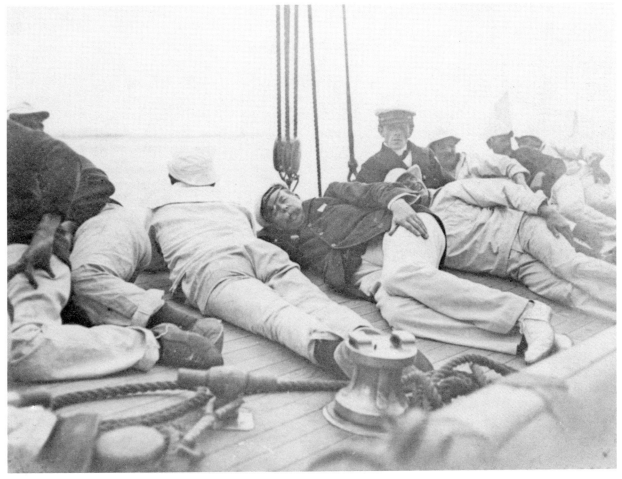

Lipton and the crew on deck of Shamrock II.

He had already shown a certain independence of mind. Thus Edward was strongly pro-French where his parents had been decidedly pro-German. He relied on businessmen such as Lipton and bankers like Cassel for information about the United States. However paradoxical it was, there was a sense in which he liked what he had heard of the more classless and relaxed U.S.A.

The second challenge by Lipton with the yacht *Shamrock II* almost deprived Great Britain of her monarch before he had time to accustom himself to the throne. He had gone down to the Solent with his friend and mistress, Mrs. Alice Keppel, to see the trials of the new yacht which had been built on the Clyde at Dumbarton by Denny Brothers, whose yard had produced the famous clipper *Cutty Sark*. Despite his outspoken comments at the time of his first challenge, Lipton had had perforce to go back to George Watson as designer.

The King was aboard the yacht when a sudden squall brought the mainmast toppling to the deck, missing him by a comparatively narrow margin. He seems to have behaved with generous concern and a real coolness, asking only if anyone had been hurt. He is also supposed to have shown a nimble turn of wit when he asked if the boom was still intact. On being told that it was, he is supposed to have rejoined "How very singular! If the boom did not suffer how are we to account for the collapse of Sir Thomas's sales?"

The mishap left Lipton depressed and mortified but the King tried hard to console and re-assure him. The two men undoubtedly had a certain rapport and Lipton's position was strengthened when he found a well-paid place in the American department of his organisation for Mrs. Keppel's husband, George, which would conveniently remove Keppel from the scene of action. The *Philadelphia Times* with either an unwonted naivete or its tongue lodged far back in its cheek commented:- "The handsome appointment which Sir Thomas Lipton has given to Mr. George Keppel is very agreeable to the Prince who is much interested in the family".

Lipton lost no chance to assert openly that he was certain of receiving fair treatment from the Americans. "As in business, so in sport" was a much-used phrase of his. He resisted the temptation to rise to the bait he was sometimes offered. After his first defeat the American magazine The *World* had presented a barbed little poem to its readers:-

While on the triangular course you declare
As straight as an arrow your rival you found,
It's curious to hear your defeat was all square
When we'd the idea you were beaten all round.

He was not beaten all round in 1901 although defeat was once again his portion. *Shamrock II*, well captained by Edward Sycamore from Brightlingsea, won the first race, and over the whole series there was only three minutes and twenty-seven seconds difference between the times of the yachts, *Columbia* again defending for the Americans.

Sir Thomas could be depended upon to find the felicitous phrase. He reminded his listeners that the shamrock to be perfect had three leaves and that he would be back. A New York newspaper made a friendly enquiry as to whether such a shamrock outbid a four-leaf clover which the Americans claimed to have in abundance. Sir Thomas maintained that he would be back and back moreover on his own:- "The next *Shamrock* will not be the product of a combine or a committee or the mixture of a dozen different ideas. She'll be mine, every spar of her". He would never have agreed to be part of a team

Departure for America. Shamrock III being taken in tow by the Flying Phantom alongside Gourock Pier. May 1903.

The Juno, specially chartered by the Lord Provost of Glasgow and friends to give a hearty send-off to Shamrock III. 28th May 1903.

Guests on the Erin watching the races.

Prince Joseph De Croy, Prince Reginald De Croy, Thomas Edison and Sir Thomas Lipton with guests on the Erin. 5th October 1899.

to recover the Cup; apart from anything else, there would be no percentage in it for him.

In his preparation for the third attempt on the America's Cup Lipton had no greater well-wisher than the King and just before he sailed he was the recipient of the following royal telegram:-

Windsor Castle

As you are just about leaving for the U.S.A. let me wish you a prosperous journey and all possible good luck for the great race in August.

Edward, King Emperor

The King's friendship did not mean that this new challenge would come from the Royal Yacht Squadron. Once again Lipton's device would be that of the Royal Ulster Yacht Club and the background to this is rather turgid. As far back as

August 1900 the *Daily Chronicle* had carried the following paragraph.

"I hear that Sir Thomas Lipton is a candidate for admission to the Royal Yacht Squadron on the personal nomination of the Prince of Wales. Balloting takes place tomorrow and it is not doubted that Sir Thomas will be unanimously elected".

The *Freeman's Journal* of the same date certainly doubted it and, as it turned out, with good reason.

"It is often found that despite such backing these candidates fare badly at the hands of old fogies who regard every new candidate as an intruder. The fact that the Prince of Wales will be absent from the meeting may also adversely affect the issue in what is one of the most narrowly exclusive clubs in the world".

So, was Sir Thomas Lipton a formal candidate for admission to the Royal Yacht Squadron and was he blackballed, thus inflicting a snub not only upon himself but on his royal sponsor? It very much seemed to depend upon which newspapers one read. The *Morning Leader* of the following day August 7th, left it to the reader to learn by inference:- "Lord Cawdor withdrew his own nomination since his boat was too small and another candidate failed to be elected". A week later the *Birmingham Argus* was more downright:-

"Sir Thomas Lipton has been blackballed and the Prince of Wales is so wrathful that he has boycotted all social inter-course with the Royal Yacht Squadron".

This was in flat contradiction to the *Commercial Advertiser* which declared:-

"Sir Thomas Lipton was never a formal candidate for admission to the Royal Yacht Squadron. He was given to understand that his nomination would be opposed and he withdrew. We gather that what stood against him was that he was a yacht owner but not a practical yachtsman".

This last has the genuine ring to it. If Lipton had learned that he would be opposed, and one black ball would have done it, then it made sense to spare himself the public rebuff. He remained touchy about the issue, to the extent that he threatened libel action against any publication which spread the story that he had actually been blackballed. It may seem strange that the royal influence did not avail him but the Squadron would very much have regarded the King as a member like any other and resented any attempt to fill it with the King's friends.

As we have seen, Edward was more open than his most aristocratic subjects but he had to give way also on the subject of a possible peerage for the Scot two years after the business of the Royal Yacht Squadron. The Prime Minister of the day, the Marquis of Salisbury, absolutely refused to consider Lipton for anything more than a baronetcy, the lowest order of hereditary title and this is what was conferred. The Prime Minister was actually quoted as saying in the *Philadelphia American* that "the hereditary peerage has been sufficiently debauched of late". It has to be said of Salisbury that he could claim a certain kind of consistency, for he himself declined a dukedom, on the grounds that the marquisate which he held was infinitely older and more distinguished.

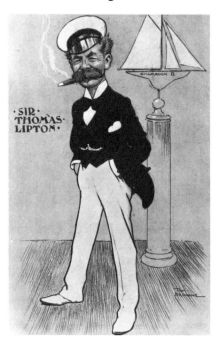

Lipton again moved quickly to defuse the situation. To the sister Philadelphia newspaper, the *Inquirer* he stated:- "A peerage has not been offered me and, if it should be I, while appreciating the great honour, would be compelled to decline. I have no desire to get so far away from my friends and am satisfied to remain as I am". There may have been a shrewd realisation here that although a title might have helped him in Britain it could have been something of an albatross in the United States.

No title, and again in 1903 no America's Cup. *Shamrock III* had again been built by Denny Brothers of Dumbarton although this time the design of the yacht was back with William Fife. There was a new captain, Robert Wringe of Southampton who had been second-in command on the first of the name. Once again the condition that the challenger must cross the Atlantic by her own efforts had loaded the dice too heavily against the visitors. What was good enough in trials on this side of the ocean did not stand up in competition.

The third series was one-sided to the point of being almost boring. As the contest grew ever more legalistic there was now a rough weather provision which would in certain circumstances stop racing. Even some of the Americans, responsible for the introduction of the saving clause privately thought that this was an absurd concept given the amount of money and labour that went into such boats, especially when the challenger was required to cross the Atlantic under her own power. The American defender *Reliance* had proved her superiority at every turn and it was no consolation for Lipton to be continually told that he had a beautiful boat. Just for a moment there was the slightest of chips in the veneer of the world's most sporting loser. "I don't want a beautiful boat. I want a homely boat that'll win. I want *Reliance*".

Already he was turning his mind to another attempt but this time he would insist that the yachts should be of the same dimensions, to unload the dice as it were. On his way back to Britain on the transatlantic liner he could while the time away by taking out the *Erin's* Visitors Book and reflecting that his ship's decks had welcomed Thomas Alva Edison, Henry Ford, Pierpont Morgan and the President himself, Theodore Roosevelt. In the great scales of life that ought to outweigh a Yacht Squadron membership denied and a peerage refused.

He would be back, but not immediately. For a variety of reasons it would be the other side of the Kaiser's War before the by now almost traditional rivalry was renewed. By then Lipton would be relatively more important in American life than in his native country.

Sir Thomas Lipton, Admiral Dewey, Oliver Iselin, General Chaffee, Hon. W.H. Moody(Secretary United States Navy),President Roosevelt,and Mrs Roosevelt on board the Mayflower.

CHAPTER 9
FULL FLOWERING

The first decade of the new century saw Lipton at the height of his commercial achievement and it was a time moreover when he was beginning to shed some of his austere and even monastic habits of life. He was an assured friend of the new King; when the latter took seriously ill and in consequence there had to be a postponement of his Coronation, Lipton was one of the comparatively few who called at the Palace to express his concern personally.

Shortly we will look at Lipton's new-found interests but it is important to establish that he had retained all his old commercial acumen. The most potent demonstration of this came in the United States where in the autumn of 1900 he cornered the pork market by a series of astute moves. He had realised that the Spanish-American War and the Boer War, being fought virtually at the same time, would put severe pressure on the market to supply both armies with canned pork. By October 1900 he had effectively cornered the market and the price of pork had shot up from 11 to 17 dollars a barrel. Over that barrel he now literally held his competitors and by the standards and indeed expectations of the time he could have exacted a very heavy price from them indeed. The market had been anxiously watching the traditionally great houses of Armour and Cudahy and while they did so Lipton had come up on the outside.

As with Abraham Lincoln's method in politics, Lipton's inclination was to "let them up lightly". He could have plucked a figure from the sky and those of his competitors already contracted to "sell on" would have had no alternative but to pay up.

Lipton, perhaps out of mischief, at first maintained that this happy state of affairs had come about by accident rather than through some brilliant grand design. He let it be widely known that he would release substantial quantities of pork to the southern states because he felt strongly that negroes should not have to pay eight cents a pound for spare ribs.

Eventually he admitted what everybody already knew, that he had contracted for all the available pork. He moved swiftly to deflect any possible criticism:

"I have no intention of raising prices to an exorbitant degree. I am perfectly satisfied to make simply a fair profit out of all my dealings and will do everything possible to avoid causing serious trouble to those who sold short. In fact I let some go the other day to save a few threatened failures".

Possibly out of courtesy, the impending failures were not specified. The Chicago Post, in a line which it most surely should have resisted, declaimed "This goes to show that a man

Top. Lipton on horseback at Osidge.

Bottom. Sir Thomas Lipton's Daimler and Panhard motor cars in front of his residence at Osidge. He kept a fleet of cars for sport and for the use of his guests.

who has cornered the pork market need not be hoggish". As ever Lipton had miraculously combined philanthropy with a good press and a handsome profit. By selling at $17 dollars per barrel having bought on at 11 dollars, he cleared more than $300,000 dollars on the transaction and there was another America's Cup challenger paid for.

There was a balancing act to be done here. Lipton was not so naive as not to know that, despite his personal amiability and the affection that the Americans genuinely felt for him, there might be a counter-coup. He had been coming round to the notion that the Chicago Packing House was really too far away from the rest of the operation to receive the consistent rigorous scrutiny that it needed. He had long since abandoned any idea of extending the retail side of his operation to America and it made sense to quit the pork production business at the top. He therefore sold out to Armour for $250,000 dollars and effectively left the meat-packing trade.

Back home he took good care that a high profile should be maintained. He subscribed £1000 to the memorial for Queen Victoria. He suddenly acquired an interest in Association Football. In April 1901 he attended the international match at Crystal Palace between England and Scotland and all through the 2-2 draw vigorously encouraged the Scots. When, in the return match at Ibrox Park Glasgow, the following year, part of the terracing gave way and scores of spectators were killed he was quick to send a cheque for the relief of the families of the victims. The week after he was back at Crystal Palace for the Cup Final between Sheffield United and Southampton. The crowd recognised him and surrounded him, cheering and singing "Good Old *Shamrock*", but although he doffed his hat civilly in acknowledgement for once he could not be persuaded to speak to them.

He was very open to inventions. His pride and joy had been his fast carriage horses but this was the age of the car and he embraced it eagerly. He had had a fine stable of horses, now he would have many cars. He had driven his own horses for pleasure, now he would master his Mercedes, his Daimler, his Panhard 22 h.p. He was a dashing rather than a good driver. Before long he had been fined for speeding and had driven into railings in Woodford.

Much more serious was his car accident at Alresford near Winchester. A carter named Bright was leading a horse which bolted when Lipton's car passed close to it. Lipton appears to have left the scene and Bright was found dead with a fractured skull. At the inquest the Coroner, Henry White, was very curt in his treatment of Lipton and clearly felt that considerable blame attached to him. Lipton appeared in person and in the course of his evidence promised to do the best he possibly could for the dependents of the deceased. At once the Coroner forbade him to touch upon this subject and he was equally quick to intervene when, at the end of the proceedings, Lipton attempted to thank the jury for their verdict which effectively exculpated him.

By this time he had a box at Covent Garden but makes no reference to ever having attended a particular performance. He does not appear to have felt the need to supply the inevitable cultural deficiencies of his early education. There was no attempt to read himself towards intellectuality and even had the wish been there the time was not.

The temptation would be to say that he was not a man in whom the aesthetic instinct was strongly developed but occasionally he puts the case for his own defence and it is only fair to read what he says, although with the qualification that he said it in an interview, where often the first consideration was to supply a struggling reporter with good colour. Thus, in August 1903, in the run-up to the races of that year, he mentions to a New York woman reporter that he had at one time been a competent violinist:

"I could read and execute admirably considering the time I studied. The violin is a good tranquilliser but it cannot bring quick results. I studied it with a German teacher". He would almost certainly have admitted that he was happier with the songs of the other world-renowned Scot of the time, Harry Lauder.

This was a fruitful time for Lipton with only two wispy clouds in the sky, the changed atmosphere in his business, and the alarming deterioration in the health of the King.

The drawing room of Lipton's palatial steam yacht Erin.

Lipton was now well into his fifties but his physical vigour and his business acumen were totally undiminished. There is now, however, a change in the pattern of his life with perhaps two months of assiduous daily attendance at his place of business often followed by an absence of almost the same duration. A physical absence only, because he would be on to his headquarters dozens of times in a day, demanding information, conveying information and seeking assurances that all was well. Even when apparently pleasure-cruising in the *Erin*, local agents never knew the moment when his tall spare figure would walk in the door and conduct a searching enquiry on the current state of affairs.

It was well for him that he knew how to keep the common touch for he was certainly walking a lot with kings. His friendship with Edward VII had catapulted him into a whole new world and he was now an accepted member of Europe's aristrocatic yachting community. He loved travelling and cruised for months in successive seasons in the Meditteranean entertaining royalty and procession of illustrious men and women from all walks of life on board his luxurious steam yacht the *Erin*. In April 1904 he was cruising in the Mediterranean, calling at Nice and Cannes and shortly afterwards he was the guest of King Victor Emmanuel II of Italy at the royal palace in Naples. Before he left he found himself a Knight Commander of the Order of the Crown of Italy. In May of that year he was happy to make the *Erin* available to the ex-Empress of France, Eugenie, to enable her to visit Marseilles.

He concluded his spell away from the office by going to Kiel in Germany to race in the famous Kiel Week, where of course the Kaiser was the leading luminary. Wilhelm II may have dismissed him earlier as "my uncle's grocer" but relations were much warmer between the two men now, since Lipton had executed one of those tactical withdrawals at which he was so very adept. He himself had wished to present a trophy for competition by yachtsmen for Transatlantic racing. On hearing that the same idea had apparently occurred to the Kaiser at much the same time, Lipton cheerfully declared that he would be honoured to withdraw in favour of the German Emperor.

Europe was all very well, but Lipton's heart was genuinely engaged elsewhere. He had realised that his profile was inevitably slightly lowered by his withdrawal from the pork business in the United States. It had become evident too that this might not have been a decision entirely of his own making. The *Chicago Examiner* was emphatic that the National Packing Company - an amalgam of the three great canned meat firms of Armour, Swift and Morris - had consciously decided to absorb all the smaller packing concerns.

The entertaining Sir Thomas.

Below. Lipton on the Shamrock with King Alfonso of Spain and his party.

Above. Lipton entertains the monks of Iveron Monastery while on a Meditteranean cruise, April1900.

Below. Presentation of the freedom of the Borough of Erin.

Just at the moment it was inconvenient to visit the United States in person so he came up with an astute answer. The U.S.S. *Olympia* was coming on a good will visit to Britain and he would entertain 500 of her crew. He would do it at the Crystal Palace, and he would do it moreover on Trafalgar Day. He spared no expense to entertain them lavishly. This was the menu:-

Mock Turtle Soup
Turbot, Hollandaise Sauce
Mutton Cutlets Reforme
Surrey Chicken
Brussels Sprouts, Potatoes, Salad
Xmas Pudding, Fruit Tart
Cheese, Coffee
Claret, Beer, Mineral Waters

The sailors doubtless most appreciated the last-named since, unlike their British counterparts, American ships were "dry" while at sea. Lipton presided in his inimitable amiable manner and made his usual little speech about still being in contention for the America's Cup. He must have been gratified by the stentorian shouts of "You deserve it" from the grateful but unpatriotic tars.

He was very much still regarded as amongst the first flight of entrepreneurs. When he visited Ceylon in early 1905 after an absence of several years, it was in reality nothing more than check on the state of his concerns there. However, this was not nearly satisfactory for the press who would have nothing else than that a burgeoning interest in the rubber business had taken him there. They had not given up on him as a fertile source of news and he did not disappoint them on this occasion either. No rubber involvement, but he was going to open a shop in Paris, in the Place de l'Opera no less.

A few months later, in September 1905 he survived a potentially serious mishap. In his capacity as Honorary Colonel of the Second Volunteer Battalion, Highland Light Infantry (often referred to as the Lanark Engineers) he was on horseback at the head of his men when just as he was passing before the King who was on the saluting base at Holyrood Park, Edinburgh, his mount threw him and in falling his head was cut quite deeply by the flailing hooves of his horse. He insisted on walking off unaided for treatment and a couple of days of rest put him to rights.

It is doubtful whether he would have appreciated the alleged quote in the *Sheffield Independent* that "Sir Thomas owns that he is safer in a boat than in the pigskin" but he himself did say that "before starting I should have made myself better acquainted with the circus business".

The King enquired anxiously after his health as he was due to join the Royal Family at Balmoral in October, an engagement he was happily able to keep. He observed His Majesty, whose bulk made him a somewhat unlikely dancer, took part in several of the dances, though not the "ferocious eightsomes, which His Majesty was happy to leave to the younger set" as *The Scotsman* loyally put it. His waltzing with Mrs. George Keppel was much admired.

He got home to England to find that another ghost had been raised, the connection of the company with the Irish Home Rule movement. One of the most prominent of Irish Nationalist M.P.s Michael Davitt, had just died and it came out that at the time of the flotation of the company Lipton had allocated, gratis, 1000 of his own shares to Davitt. His explanation was that at the time the M.P., who was one-armed since a childhood accident and therefore had much employment closed to him, was in straitened circumstances and that the share allocation was simply an attempt to ease his financial crisis.

Curiously it would not be the Irish connection that landed Lipton in a major difficulty, but a pillar of the establishment, the Army. The business had strong military links by this time; it provisioned the Volunteer camps which had now become Territorial Army, and it was responsible for the victualling during the large-scale manoeuvres which took place every summer on Salisbury Plain. Moreover, it tendered regularly for the privilege of supplying the canteens of those units stationed abroad.

In theory, various firms tendered to supply regimental canteens and the colonel of the regiment decided who should fulfil the order. In practice, the contracts depended largely on word-of-mouth recommendations from the senior N.C.O.s, the quartermasters, the regimental sergeant-majors and the cooks. It was the local Lipton agent's job to keep these men sweet, quite an arduous task in well-garrisoned bases such as Gibraltar or Malta.

It was a system greatly open to abuse and a dissatisfied Lipton employee who had jumped ship over a question of salary and gone to work for the competing Canteen Mess Society now decided to make trouble. He had signed an agreement not to work for any competing firm for a year after leaving Lipton (fairly standard practice at the time) but broke this agreement and Lipton sued for breach of contract.

It would have been wiser to let Mr. Evans (the name of the employee) go, for he was of little account. His dismissal brought such matters as his salary under scrutiny and it became clear that much of his salary had been in the form of "expenses" for his agents to pass on to influential N.C.O.s. Among these agents was a Colonel Savage, who while in command in Malta had been receiving £300 per year, paid to him by Lipton's Malta agent, Mr. Morris. It speedily became apparent that the current canteen system in the British Army was dependent on bribery, pure and simple.

These events had taken place eleven years previously and Colonel Savage maintained that he had not been paid for showing favour where his own regimental canteen was concerned, but for previous services rendered in Crete and Cyprus at a time when he was on leave, and there was no bar on him doing so.

The case was held at the Central Criminal Court in London before Mr. Justice Darling, who seemed as much aghast at the social rank of those involved as at the actual question of inducement. The nub of the case for Lord Darling was that a Colonel should have conspired with a tradesman to accept money so that he could show favour or disfavour to a commercial firm in relation to catering contracts with his regiment. The wretched Colonel Savage received six months imprisonment but much more damaging for Sir Thomas Lipton were the last few sentences of Lord Darling's judgment. "I am satisfied from the evidence before the court that those defendants employed by Lipton's, in so far as they made payment for the profits of persons who were capable of influencing contracts in favour of Lipton's, were acting upon a system which was known to the directorate, encouraged by the directorate and persisted in by the directorate".

As it happened the Annual General Meeting of Shareholders took place only a week afterwards. Lipton skimmed over the whole affair. It had all happened some years ago, which was true, and the practice had now been given up, which was also true. It had been on a pitifully small scale anyway, in a balance sheet of millions one was talking about a few thousand pounds.

The audience was not convinced. When Lipton mentioned new directors being brought on to the Board there was a low growl of approval and cries of "We need 'em!" For the first time his own total commitment to the company was questioned: "Attend to your business and leave yachting alone". This hostile intervention was the saving of him because a well-wisher immediately yelled out "never mind the dividends, bring us back the cup!" Lipton craftily took this as an expression of the general feeling of the meeting, which assuredly it was not and declared that the adoption of the report had been carried unanimously, when it most patently had not been.

He was not as blase as he appeared to be. He felt the sting of public rebuke keenly. Till now he could identify himself with Captain Corcoran in *H.M.S. Pinafore*:

I have lived hitherto
Free from the breath of slander
Beloved by all my crew
A really popular commander

He had no personal involvement, but he knew that this could not exculpate him. His was the name above the door; he should have been aware of what was going on. The fact that the Army was involved was a bitter blow to him as Honorary Colonel. A major consolation was that his friend, Edward VII had not lived to witness his discredit.

Edward VII died in the summer of 1910 and with a whimsical aptness, the last information that he was able to comprehend was that his horse, Witch of the Air, had won that afternoon at Kempton Park. It was some slight consolation for his ever-growing belief that the British throne would be swept aside in the tide of republicanism then engulfing Europe.

He was wrong about that but the accession of George V brought to an end those days in which Sir Thomas Lipton had been a regular part of the court circle. It was not that the new monarch was hostile, rather the old axiom that to be in at court in one reign was to be out in the next. In a way it was odd that he, in whom the puritanical streak was by no means absent, should have been spiritually more at home with the raffish Edward than the dutiful George. George V was the first monarch to work consciously at the idea of the "happy family" for public consumption. In fact his quarterdeck manner meant that life at the Palace was excessively formal and his children chafed under innumerable restrictions but his subjects did not know that. Lipton too was now 60 and inevitably reflected the virtues and failings of the previous generation.

That, together with the admonition received in the Army Canteen affair, although in reality a slap on the wrist, led to his adopting a slightly lower profile in the first few years of the new reign. The friends of Edward were viewed with a certain amount of suspicion and the new King, with his naval background, did not find the company of bankers and self-made men as congenial as had his father.

Lipton missed his direct involvement in major American commerce. On his estates in Ceylon he entertained two leading baseball sides, the Chicago White Sox and the New York Giants, and once again genuine good-heartedness would be happily married to keeping his name before the American public. His feeling for the United States went far beyond a vague philanthropy.

He could think as an American. He was totally free of the condescension which bedevilled the Foreign Office approach. Whitehall had the notion that although the Americans were destined to cut the larger figure on the world stage in future, British cultural superiority would be able to keep the young Abners docile. This was a British delusion which would persist to the time of Kennedy and McMillan with the older man foolishly imagining that he could play the Greek to the other's Roman. Lipton could see, patriot though he was, that on some points of foreign policy the Americans might well be right, and although a certain amount of self-interest was involved there was also the capacity to take the wider view.

It was time to take up again the challenge for the America's Cup. He was unable to persuade the New York Yacht Club to do away with time allowances, which would always favour the defender but he had *Shamrock IV* built at Portsmouth in conditions of great secrecy. Just occasionally this most level-headed of men could do something quite bizarre and he insisted that every man who worked on the building of the boat should be a bachelor. The fear, which Lipton was injudicious enough to articulate, was that married men would gossip to their wives about construction details which were secret.

The races were scheduled for the autumn of 1914. As *Shamrock IV* crossed the Atlantic at the beginning of August the accompanying *Erin* picked up by radio a message from a German cruiser which made it plain that war had broken out between Britain and Germany. Lipton stayed in the States just long enough to lay up *Shamrock IV* at a Brooklyn yard and then he returned to England. It would be six years before the keel of *Shamrock* would touch the water in serious competition.

CHAPTER 10
THE LAST VOYAGE OF THE ERIN

The cataclysmic outburst of August 1914 made it certain that the Canteen scandal would be interred with the bodies of the first fallen soldiers. Lipton lost the sense of faintly uneasy drift of which he had begun to be conscious. The country could surely now use his organisational skills and if it needed prompting to do so, he would supply the prompting.

The Erin at Monte Carlo.

Immediately he made the *Erin* available as a hospital ship and in conjunction with the Duchess of Westminster he transported a complete field hospital to France. This was well-meant but not the answer he sought. Public opinion even thus early in the war was not enamoured of society women who tiptoed prettily around the battlefield as in pre-war days they would have taken soup to the poor of London's East End. The war was scarcely a couple of months old but it was clear that grim, unremitting professionalism was the only thing that could bring it to a successful conclusion.

His second venture with the *Erin* was better judged. Serbia was being fiercely beset by the superior forces of Austria-Hungary. It was a cause which particularly appealed to Scots. Several women doctors went out from Scotland, among them the celebrated Elsie Inglis from Edinburgh. Lipton decided to make the *Erin* available to ferry seven surgeons, three nurses and three orderlies who had been enlisted by the Order of St John of Jerusalem and the British Red Cross.

Even yet, there was the last despairing cry of pre-1914 society. The first port of call was Monte Carlo where, to the great indignation of the medical staff, the Casino refused them

Above. Nurses embarking at Marseilles for Serbia.

Below. Innoculating the nurses against typhoid.

admission because they were dressed in uniform. No one who knew the grim work which lay ahead of them would with hindsight have grudged them a last few hours of relaxation.

At Athens there was a masked ball, attended by the King and Queen of Greece, soon to be exiled, and a fair sprinkling of Czarist Russian nobility, most of whom would soon be dead. Then the *Erin* threaded its way through the Corinth Canal and in doing so had reached the theatre of war. Lipton went on to Belgrade and watched the Austrian shelling of that city alongside Prince Paul, who was to be regent after the murder of King Alexander in Marseilles some twenty years later.

Soon the English press carried photographs of this event, "Lipton under Fire", "Displays coolness during shelling". The real work was about to start at the town of Nish. Here the main danger to the populace was neither shot nor shell but a virulent outbreak of typhus against which two medical units, one British and one American (the United States was still of course a neutral country at this stage) were heroically but short-handedly striving.

Now Lipton was invaluable. He could be, and was, accused of an excessive desire for publicity on occasions but in such cases there was no one like him. If he appeared with Serbian Generals in flamboyant uniforms or on the decks of the now red-cross *Erin*, he was demonstrating that here was a civilian population in desperate need. A grateful Serb government made him a Grand Commander of the Order of St. Sava.

He was particularly struck by the heroic work being done by Dr. James Donnelly, of the American Red Cross Mission. He asked Lipton if he had such a thing as a very large American flag which might avert the hostile attentions of the contending forces. Lipton immediately handed over one which he kept on board the *Erin*. It was designed to meet a melancholy need for a short time later Dr. Donnelly succumbed to the disease and his body was buried wrapped in the Stars and Stripes. His death affected Lipton profoundly and when eventually he returned to the United States at the end of the war he made a point of meeting the widowed Mrs. Donnelly and of providing for her young son's education.

He himself toyed with the notion of going over to America to put the British point of view and there was no-one from whom it would have been more readily received. He was not sure, however, that this might not be construed as deserting his post, and decided against it. Another consideration was that he was the driving force of an enormous business concern and therefore had a duty not to hazard himself on a submarine-infested ocean.

The Erin passing through Corinth Canal.

Lipton's task was ready-delineated for him, to take the place once more of the young men who were enlisting. As he was a Volunteer Colonel, he could not possibly stop his young men from going to France. In the stir of coping with this enormous emergency he found himself again. He became a lavish contributor to Forces comforts and charities; if the crates of food donated to the troops still carried the stenciller's handwork that mattered little to those soldiers who received them.

He had been to Serbia when many a 64 year old would have stayed at home. And he had no reason to be ashamed of the publicity he had generated which eventually brought the typhus epidemic under control. He was now about to donate something to the war effort which cost him more than mere money ever could.

German U-boats were making severe inroads into British shipping in late 1915 and the Government was glad to take replacements wherever they might be offered. He now stated that he would hand the *Erin* over to the Admiralty for patrol work and in doing so she resumed her original name, *Aegusa*. She was not destined to have a long Royal Navy career as she was sunk in June 1916 and the waters of the Mediterranean finally closed over those decks which had once rung to the feet of the most important men and women in Europe and America. Several of the crew perished with her, all known to Lipton, and it was as near to a personal bereavement as an old and solitary man could experience.

His role was that of encourager. He entertained servicemen on leave at Osidge, kicked-off at big football matches, the Government looking favourably on these because in the days of volunteering they were excellent recruiting grounds for Flanders. In a sense he was back where he had been before he ventured into society some twenty years before. If it did nothing else it silenced those few gnat-like shareholders who wished him to spend more time on business matters.

Crisis threatened in early 1918 with the introduction of the Conscription Act. Suddenly, France and Mesopotamia was not an option, but a command. If the war lasted the only answer was the large-scale introduction of women into mens' jobs, and even more trickily, posts of responsibility. He was in the middle of considering these developments when the sudden end to the war made such deliberations unnecessary.

He was without close kin and so had nobody to lose to the dreadful carnage which characterised that war to end wars. Yet he was saddened by the number of younger employees who lost their lives when caught up in the enthusiasm of volunteering.

He was given, moreover, a macabre insight into what it meant to have a close relative at the front.

He learned one day of the death in action of Captain John Lauder, the son of Harry Lauder the Scottish comedian, a friend of long-standing. It was over the Christmas period of 1917 which made the loss all the more poignant. Lipton with considerable hesitation and dread lifted the telephone to offer his condolences. To his horror it became apparent from the carefree greeting of Harry Lauder that he had not yet been informed of the death of his son. In an agony of indecision Lipton debated with himself whether it was his place to break the news of the boy's death.

He finally decided against doing this, and muttering the conventional greetings of the season, put the phone down, leaving his fellow-Scot to enjoy the last couple of hours of happiness that he was likely to know. Well, that was behind him now and it would fall to him to do what he could to help make "a land fit for heroes to live in" as the cant phrase of the time had it. He was the more willing to do this as he came up to the Biblical span of his age; it would give him a sense of purpose for however long he had left to him.

Sir Thomas with Dr. Donnelly, who tragically fell victim to typhus.

Ship on fire at Salonika harbour.

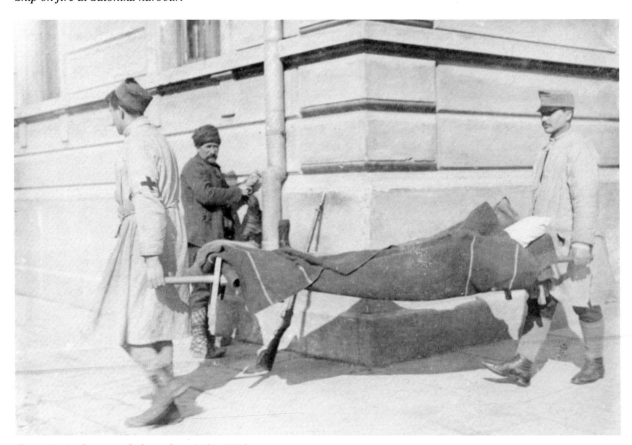

Carrying in the wounded at a hospital in Nish.

Unloading the cars at Salonika.

At Berry's Hospital, Vrnyetska Banja.

113

The great delusion about wars is that they are almost always fought to restore things to where they were. So it was with the Great War of 1914. Emperors fell, Germany and Russia became, for the moment at least, almost powerless. Even the victors themselves, France, Britain and the United States did not emerge unaffected. There was no longer the same unquestioning acceptance that the freedom of energetic and unscrupulous businessmen to amass very large fortunes was necessarily something which contributed to the public good. From now on their behaviour would be subjected to increasingly closer public scrutiny. The lavish expenditure of Edwardian times, which had seemed the natural course for rich men, would now provoke at best censure and at worst overt hostility.

This change in attitude did not of course occur over a weekend and there was a natural attempt made to get back to those pre-war days of low taxation and lax business laws. For the first time in five years Lipton beheld the famous set-piece of the Manhattan sky-line as his ship sailed into New York harbour. Prominent on that skyline were his new and grander premises in Hoboken; no arriving or departing passenger who could read would be unaware that in this commercial paradise he was a major player.

He lost no time in checking out *Shamrock IV* which had spent the last five years or so tied up in a Brooklyn boatyard. She was in good shape and preparations were made for a crew of Essex fishermen to come over and join the skipper, the celebrated amateur yachtsman Sir W.P. Burton. It seemed an odd choice to pit this collection of unproven amateurs against the highly professional crew of the defender *Resolute*, men who were virtually all on permanent retainers, but in fact *Shamrock IV* was to come closer to success than any other of Sir Thomas Lipton's ventures.

The British yacht won the first two races and crossed the line ahead of her rival in the third, but the time allowance tipped the scales in favour of the Americans. *Resolute* won the fourth race and matters were square at two all. The morning of the fifth race was distinctly blowy, something that could only work to the advantage of the more stoutly-built British boat. Lipton was jubilant. His elation was not long-lasting for almost in the same moment he was aware that the flag was being flown which signified that conditions were too hazardous for racing.

For almost the first time his celebrated sangfroid deserted him. The wind speed was estimated at 25 knots and he was not alone in thinking that racing was perfectly feasible. The great American sports writers, Damon Runyon and Ring Lardner, had always been inclined to take rather a detached view of the whole

Opposite. Sir Thomas Lipton with Mrs. James Donnelly and her son. Lipton became the sponsor of the young boy following the death of his father, Dr. Donnelly, from typhus during the Serbian war.

Overleaf. Sir Thomas Lipton on board Shamrock IV.

Overleaf. Sir Thomas Lipton and the crew of Shamrock IV in dry dock before the race.

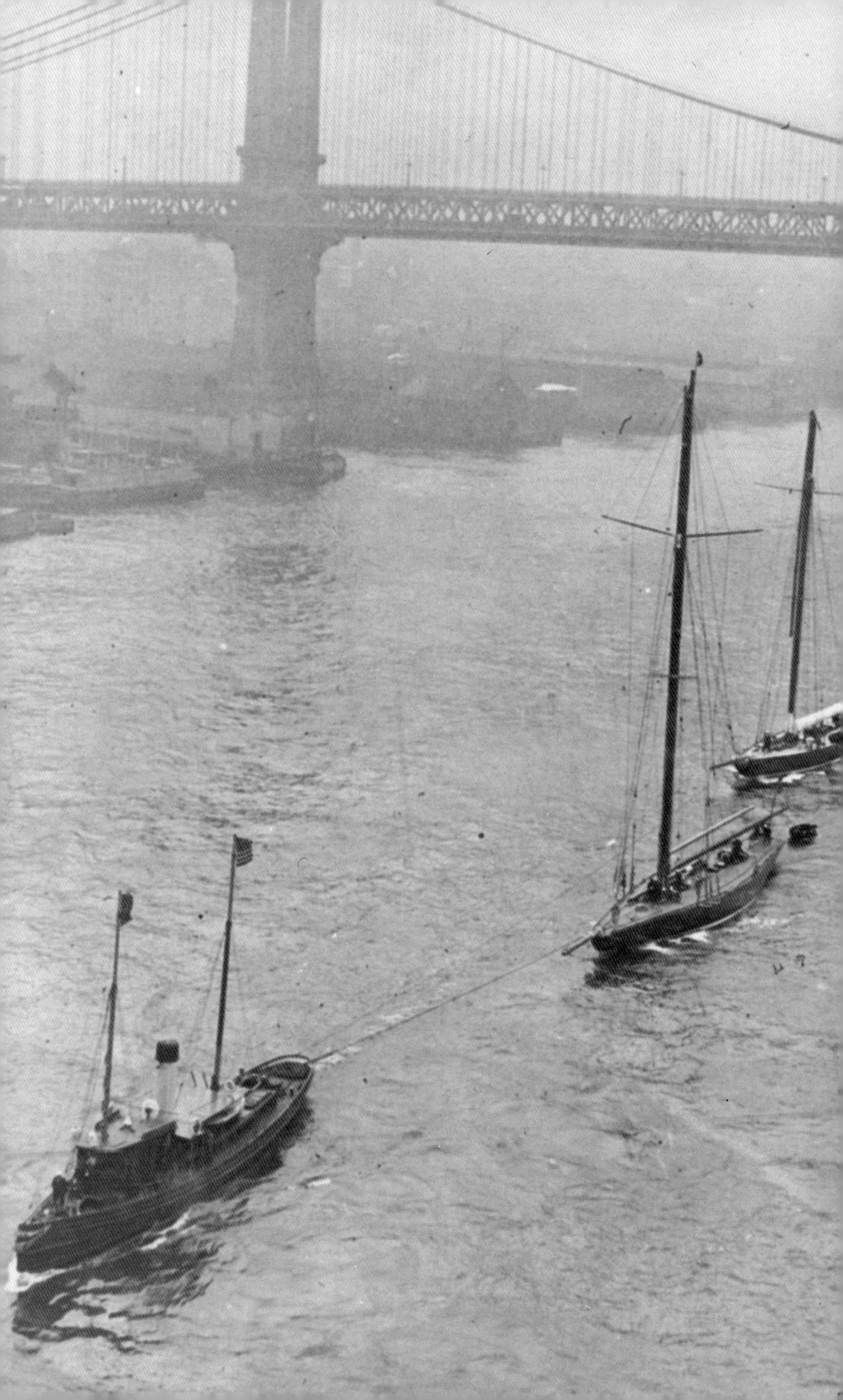

America's Cup business. They had pointed out how fundamentally uninteresting to the average man such contests were. With every race it seemed that there was always either a flat calm or the sea was too rough. What was the point of spending hundreds of thousands of dollars on boats which were unable to sail in sheltered waters in breezes as gentle as 12 knots?

Surprisingly, Lipton's anger was short-lived and he sanctioned the decision to abandon racing on that particular day. Here his incapacity to be angry for long let him down, for such an abandonment needed by rule the agreement of both vessels. Had Lipton insisted the race would almost certainly have gone ahead as in those circumstances *Resolute* would have had to come to the line.

As it was, *Resolute* went on to win the next race and thus complete a successful defence and for once Lipton went home feeling that he had been "suckered". Would he challenge a fifth time, the American press predictably wanted to know? A little wearily he gave his stock response that he would go back home and think about it but he would not be surprised if in the course of time he made another effort to prize the Cup away from its present holders.

Opposite. Shamrock III and IV arriving in New York.

Shamrock IV

119

LIFE HAS NOTHING MORE TO OFFER

Sir Thomas Lipton, who refused a peerage, states that appreciates no honour more than the Freedom of Glasg

Back home, another honour which he valued almost as much, more in fact if his own words can be taken at face value, came his way. This was the granting of the Freedom of Glasgow, his native city. He was installed as such in St. Andrews Hall, Glasgow, on October 2 1923 and having received his Burgess's Ticket from Lord Provost Paxton he rose to acknowledge the honour.

"This for me is the crowning distinction. Glasgow has very tender associations in my mind because it was the home of my dear parents and a home which I shared with them as long as they lived."

He went on to say that he was especially satisfied that through the agency of the *Erin* he had been able to help gallant Serbia in the War when it had been ravaged by typhus. He finished by expressing the hope that auld Glesca would enjoy continuing success.

In his speech he told some of his most celebrated tales, which were now keenly polished by repetition but over the piece he was curiously subdued. It was of course a highly-emotional occasion for there is no reason to doubt his statement that he would regard this as the greatest honour ever bestowed on him. His mind may well have gone back to his long-dead brother John, who had he lived and achieved his ambition to become a doctor, might well have been one of the distinguished audience who looked on that morning.

He was in sparkier form at the lunch when he regaled his audience with tales of his early days in America and one from that morning. Riding in the carriage to be made a Freeman he had passed by the University and had said to his companion "How well I remember passing through these buildings daily when I was a lad". The companion looked startled and disbelieving but Lipton went on:- "Surely you, of all people have not forgotten that I passed through Glasgow University? Regularly as clockwork every morning for three years I passed through it on my way to deliver groceries at the door of the kitchens which then used to be at the top of the building". He had always known what to give an audience.

It would be quite wrong to assume that Lipton spoke merely on the surface. From his own viewpoint, his attachment to Glasgow was unassailable. He had started his business there; in a very real sense Glasgow had made him what he was. By maintaining his headquarters there for 20 years he was repaying a debt, not only to his parents, but to all the citizens. And he used the lunch to recycle one of his whimsical sayings, "Only the duffers leave Glasgow, you know". As his train pulled out of Glasgow Central Station for London that night he could, and probably

did, reflect that he had been given the highest honour which his native city was empowered to grant. As the darkened streets with which he had once been daily familiar swept past his carriage window he could also marvel that he, once an unconsidered drudge, had now been honoured by the Kings of Britain, Italy and Serbia and that there was scarcely an American President of the last 20 years whom he had not known.

If the ground was beginning to shift under Lipton's feet, it is doubtful whether he recognised this just yet. On the surface all seemed tranquil. He had fallen back on Osidge, his great spiritual retreat. It was to Osidge that a handful of friends came down from London. It was there that he had working dinners with certain very senior members of staff. It was there that he would afterwards relax for an hour or two at the billiard table. He was reputed to be a very fair player although like most very powerful men it is impossible to form a correct judgement on this since many of his opponents would not have been trying over-hard to win.

Business and politics were changing. The House of Commons was filled with those whom Prime Minister Stanley Baldwin memorably described as "hard-faced men who looked as if they had done well out of the war". There was a shift too in public attitude. There was a latent antipathy towards such politicians and although it was still basically a very docile and class-conscious society there was no longer quite the unquestioning acceptance of the rich man in his castle and the poor man at the gate.

Lipton was now comfortably grooved, although still extremely fit and active for a seventy year old. He was superbly well looked after by his Cingalese servants who knew his comparatively undemanding ways and who were sufficiently exotic to impress the casual visitor. He was by now almost a professional raconteur. His stories were pleasant, never malicious, shaded to give him the best of it of course, but yet the tales of a genuinely pleasant man. If his conversation appeared self-absorbed, seldom straying, and never for long, from the state of his own enterprises, this was because he genuinely thought that his own career had been more remarkable and achieving than that of anyone else he had ever met.

There were some people who were met on level ground. He specialised in a friendly rivalry with two other Scots, Tom Dewar, the whisky baron, and Harry Lauder, the entertainer.

With Dewar competition took the form of their trying to upstage each other over the world-wide recognition of their

Opposite. Sir Thomas Lipton.

merchandise. Nothing pleased Dewar more than to find his whisky on sale where Tea Tom's product was unknown, and Lipton was similarly delighted when receiving a cable from Dewar in Africa. "Out here three pounds of your tea will buy me six wives". Lipton immediately cabled back "Am sending three parcel samples of best tea. Please arrange for samples of wives". He was at ease with Tom Dewar and another great shopman Gordon Selfridge, because they had all faced the same problems, made good and conferred benefits on their fellow citizens.

Sir Thomas Lipton (Tea Tom) and Sir Thomas Dewar (Whisky Tom) pose for the cameras with an aspiring starlet.

With Harry Lauder, the rivalry was, as might be expected, more theatrical and consisted in seeing which of them, for public consumption, could best exemplify the traditional Scottish virtue of thrift.

"The only bet I have ever made in my life was with Sir Harry Lauder. We were both going to America, he in the *Mauretania* and I on the *Baltic* and to please Harry I staked 9d against his 4d that I would be in America first. Harry beat me but it gave him some terribly anxious moments. The *Mauretania* ran into thick fog for about three days and Harry got so excited that he went down into the engine-room to urge on the stokers. Then

Opposite. Shamrock IV (left) and Resolute seen from the Victoria, USS Tuscarora, policing the course, in the foreground.

he discovered that he had lost a sixpenny piece and all the stokers stopped to help him look for the coin. Harry finally found it in his shoe. Anyway I lost and weeks afterwards I got a postcard from Honolulu asking me to let him have the 9d and the accrued interest. I wrote back to say that I had invested it for him and that he would get it and the dividends when I returned".

What a flawless piece of publicity! Lipton was linking himself with possibly the best-known entertainer in the world at that time. As far as the public was concerned everyone knew that Lauder was a tight-fisted skinflint (it was in fact merely a clever stage persona that he had adopted) but nobody could possibly believe that Lipton, who had given away millions, could be remotely miserly and so the whole notion was irresistibly comic.

Dinner given by the Atlantic Yacht Club, 13th July 1920. On the table replicas of Shamrock IV, Resolute and the America's Cup.

The coverage might be almost universally favourable, the photographs of the royalty and aristocracy of Europe might pledge undying friendship from slowly-fading photographs at Osidge, but in a strange way their problems were now his. The great question now loomed which confronts dynasties and great enterprises alike, what is to be done about the succession?

Lipton had not as yet realised the growing isolation of his position, indeed could not realise it so long as his Sunday evening companions were men such as Tom Dewar and Andrew Weir (later Lord Inverforth). But they were men of his age and

126

men of his age were dying off. These Sunday evenings strangely included a spot of hymn-singing, strangely in that in no other regard did Lipton appear to be a religious observer. Good works rather than liturgy had been his forte. Even yet he went out Sunday after Sunday with car-loads of chocolate for the children of North Mimms because a few of their number had once been kind and polite to him when his car had yet again broken down.

In the adult world he was now extremely vulnerable. There was trouble at the Shareholders Meeting of 1925 when it was disclosed that there would be no dividend paid. Of itself this was not so terrible; there was a remarkable stability in prices between the wars, so much so that the pound was actually worth more in 1938 that it had been in 1920. The passing of a dividend in one year, therefore, need not mean very much. When however the same situation recurred in 1926 matters became more serious. Was Sir Thomas still capable of exercising overall control? If not, was it because he could not delegate or was he incapable of moving with the times?

He was fortunate in that a potentially hostile meeting was skilfully defused by his vice-chairman, Sir John Ferguson, for mollifying a restless bunch of shareholders had never been a Lipton strength. This most urbane of men showed a distressing tendency to become tetchy under even legitimate questioning from shareholders. William Blackwood, the real author of "*Leaves from the Lipton Logs*", described his last days in office as "clouded by pathetic regrets and rather stupid resentments".

His regrets might have been those of an old man but we would do him less than justice to assume that they were merely those of self-interest. Lipton had firmly believed that great success brought great responsibility to a company. He had spent his working life dealing with men, not abstractions. Louis Swift ran one pork company, P.D. Armour another, while if you dealt with an automobile company you talked to Henry Ford and if steel interested you, Andrew Carnegie. These were names above the door, they would be publicly judged by what they did personally. Did they return any of their vast sums of money to the public domain? Would they treat their workers reasonably? If they were replaced, as the trend suggested, by faceless corporate bodies, then where would the philanthropists come from? He knew what working-class life was like, so too in America did Carnegie. The new generation of conglomerates of accountants and stocktakers could not possibly know.

In 1927 he was given the title of Life President and Chairman of the company, the commercial equivalent of sending a disgraced Soviet political leader to manage a power station in Siberia. Almost immediately afterwards the business was taken over by Van den Bergh and the Meadow Dairy Company. Lipton's name was still up front but his new title was as powerless as it was valueless. It was loudly stated that Sir Thomas would always be a welcome visitor to City Road but the clear implication was that he would be expected not to avail himself of his calling card too often.

His financial settlement was quite handsome; he was bought out for £750,000, but money had never been a prime consideration; even at a much earlier age, the buzz and challenge of business had always come first. He was the last man to be expected, in Dylan Thomas's phrase to "go gentle into that good night". He was not a man to settle into years of mellow decline at Osidge. His anger was the greater in that he knew his business was fundamentally sound and in this he was proved right. After a few comparatively minor adjustments the company was paying dividends again before his death in 1931.

Yet the decision to make the change was right. The business had grown well beyond the control of any one man, even such a genius as Lipton had been in his prime.

Lipton was now in the classic dilemma of the man whose work was his life and whose work had now been taken from him. He was shrewd enough to see that there was no way back, not in Britain at least, but he still retained control of the American operation. He would concentrate on that, he had no proper locus in Britain now and the Americans had always appreciated him more in any event. Of course, it was a risk, he might have lost his magic touch in appointing to subordinate posts and any man who stays in office beyond 70 is liable to do this since he is dealing effectively with the next generation but one.

The British experience had been deeply wounding. The episode of the cuttings books proves this. Since 1878 he had amassed 84 huge cuttings books, meticulously kept. If 38 newspapers reported that he had called in at Suez then there were 38 entries in the cuttings books. Now, as abruptly as they had started, they stopped.

He was still a figure of substance in the United States, but might he be forgotten there too? There was one way to remedy this possibility and in 1927 he let it be known that he was about to make the long-promised fifth challenge for the America's Cup. This time there were significant changes to the race conditions, and there would be no allowances or handicaps, the dimensions of the competing boats would be the same and already this seemed to be a victory gained for the challenger as previously the allowances had meant the difference between British victory and British defeat.

Opposite. Shamrock V.

The launch of an America's Cup contender is a protracted affair. From the issue of the challenge until the actual races three years elapsed. In between times, on a visit to the United States, Lipton broadcasting on his steam yacht's radio telephone to the World's Radio Fair was in his usual buoyant mood.

"If any of my listeners have been away from their native land for over 70 years they will well understand how eager that cup must be to get home even for a week".

He would use the intervening time well. *Shamrock V* would once more be designed by Nicholson and built at Gosport. For the launch a special train went down from London and Lady Shaftesbury was invited to do the honours. Before it crossed the Atlantic the new *Shamrock* would be tried against an elder sister, and would take on the best that Britain had to offer. Because Lipton is so indelibly associated with racing against the Americans it can easily be forgotten that he was a highly-successful competitor on this side of the Atlantic.

At the launch he had been careful to point out the change in the rules whereby both chosen boats would have to conform to similar dimensions according to Lloyds' scantling standards. He himself was now fast approaching 80 and what had started out as harmless, indeed highly profitable, sport had almost reached the stage of an obsession. If he could regain the America's Cup then there would be nothing in his life for which he had really tried that he had not brought off.

As yet the tall spare figure was almost ramrod-straight, and the yachting cap and flyaway bow tie instantly recognisable. Shortly before his departure for the United States his biographer, William Blackwood, mentioned to John Westwood, Lipton's private secretary, that there seemed no reason why he should not have a couple of challenges left in him after the current one. He was taken aback when Westwood, who knew his employer better than any man living, replied with disturbing emphasis "Sir Thomas will NEVER cross the Atlantic to challenge again".

Certainly there could not be many more chances, if any, and even Lipton was running out of mileage in being a good loser. His inborn optimism came to his aid and his countrymen were still behind him. On July 8th 1930 the Honorary Company of Fishmongers lunched him at Fishmongers Hall to honour his past achievements and to wish him success in his latest challenge. The Prince of Wales, later Edward VIII, who was then at the height of his popularity, in a brief speech conveyed the good wishes of the Royal Family. Thirty years before his grandfather, Edward VII, had expressed precisely the same sentiments.

When Lipton rose to his feet to reply, the long body uncoiling above the table in a practised, graceful gesture, he suddenly appeared to stumble in mid-sentence in his reply. After a few seconds he collected himself and carried on. The hiatus could have been caused by an understandable emotion, though perhaps it was more sinister.

In September he set off for the fray and on his arrival in the United States the younger country invigorated him as it had never failed to do. On the social round he was in great form. When a police launch came to take him to a dinner he remarked that even as a young immigrant he had never had such a reception. He endeared himself to thousands of Bostonians when, chatting with Mary Curley, daughter of that famous picaresque mayor whose exploits are recorded in *The Last Hurrah*, he remarked that he had always had the fiercest of affections for Boston ever since learning that its citizens had thrown dozens of sacks of a competitor's tea into the harbour some 150 years before.

The races would have a new venue, they would be at Newport, Rhode Island and all was set for the spectacular climax to his thirty years of challenge. He lost the first race to the defender *Enterprise* - a marvellous name for any opponent of Lipton, and the captain of the American defender was an acquaintance of long standing, Harold Vanderbilt. The second race was not even close and the following two were equally emphatic. At his fifth challenge Lipton's defeat was on a larger scale than ever before.

The reasons were not far to seek. *Enterprise* had been tried in a white-hot furnace, she was deemed the best of four similar boats prepared to repel the challenge. Economic circumstances had meant that large-scale yachting in Britain - indeed in Europe generally - had been dying since 1919 whereas in the United States it had been developing fast. Parity of size and dimension did not help when it is realised that the duralumin main mast of the *Enterprise* was 1500-2000pounds lighter than that of *Shamrock V*.

No blame whatever attached to Captain Ned Herd of *Shamrock V*. It had seen off all European opposition but on this side of the Atlantic the boat was simply not good enough. In the bitter aftermath of defeat Lipton stated that this would be his last try. The American ship had cost five times as much to build as *Shamrock's* £30,000 and it has to be remembered that there were four American boats. The cost of competing was now beyond one man, even such a very rich man as Lipton. The future in the America's Cup lay with the syndicates and for Lipton this had no attraction.

As *Enterprise* scudded downwind, leaving *Shamrock V* well astern in the last race Lipton stood impassively, his challenge in ruins, muttering to the thronging reporters "It's no good, I can't win, I can't win". He was, as ever, graciousness personified, but the old spring had gone, there could be no shrugging off a defeat of this magnitude with a laugh. He knew that there would be no more chances.

The American victory was not over-enthusiastically received in the United States. The public at large would have liked to see the old man win, rather as when English cricket was in the doldrums in the 1940s and 1950s the Australian crowds would have been happy to see at least the occasional English win. If Thomas Lipton had failed to win the America's Cup he had certainly captured the affections of the American people and that affection now took tangible form.

Sir Thomas Lipton receiving the gold loving cup from Mayor James J. Walker in New York. On the left stands John Fitzgerald, former Mayor of Boston and on the right, Barron Collier.

It was suggested that a Loving Cup be commissioned together with a donors' book and in order to give as many as possible a chance to subscribe, no single donor could contribute more than a dollar. The responses came flooding in and certain of the inscriptions in the Donors' Book have the tart humour for which New York is justly famous. The bohemian mayor of New York City, Jimmy Walker, dedicated his entry to "possibly the world's worst yacht builder but absolutely the world's most cheerful loser".

The comment appears a touch sharp perhaps, but it should be remembered that in 1930 international sport had not quite acquired the hyper-nationalistic overtones which it was later to do and that to lose an international contest was not to commit a treasonable offence. Lipton was greatly revived by this warm outpouring of admiration, to the extent that by the time he sailed back to Europe on September 30th he was beginning to drop hints that perhaps he would have one more go.

His close associates were against this, none more so than John Westwood. He feared that the old man was in danger of making himself look foolish, and he wished to spare him this for Lipton had always been a person of some dignity. He, Westwood, was the less worried though because he could not see that Lipton would have the required stamina.

His belief received a shake when in November 1930 Lipton went back to New York to receive the Loving Cup at a formal presentation. Here was an octogenarian who took Transatlantic liners much as other people hailed taxis. The cup itself was a magnificent affair, ornately scrolled and chased with an inscription reading:

"In the name of the hundreds and thousands of Yanks and well-wishers of Sir Thomas Johnstone Lipton, Bart. K.C.V.O.".

In a happy phrase Mayor Jimmy Walker declared that the trophy could not have carried more widespread affection and respect if it had come from the League of Nations. The great American humorist, Will Rogers could not be there in person, he was working on a film in Hollywood, but he sent the following cable which was read aloud to Lipton's evident delight and amusement.

"I am sorry I cannot be with you Sir Thomas, but if you have ever tried earning a living under a Republican administration you would know that you haven't got time to go gadding around. You think this is a fine cup. Say, this is nothing to the one we're going to give you when you lose next time. I am already starting on it. I love you, Sir Thomas, but I won't drink that damned tea. Come West, young man".

When Lipton rose to acknowledge the shoal of tributes the standing ovation lasted for several minutes. He ducked his head, almost abashed, in the face of such a demonstration. Then the hall fell into silence. The words came very hesitantly

"I will try again". A long pause. "Yes, I will try again". A longer pause which grew to uncomfortable, embarrassing proportions. A social nightmare loomed which was saved by the easy courtesy and quick-thinking of Jimmy Walker

"I can well understand that on such a day Sir Thomas finds it hard to speak". He reached across for the old man's speech. "His speech will sound very well in Hector Puller's English accent".

He returned to England in November 1930. Before doing so he had looked in on the American operation and pulled off a few party tricks by correctly identifying long-service employees. He whiled away part of the winter Atlantic voyage by revising his extensive list of Christmas cards, by now down to a few close friends and hundreds of business acquaintances. He had

Opposite. Lipton takes the wheel.

almost determined to go again in 1932. He remembered what he had been taught about Bruce and the spider.

There remained one honour to be garnered. Almost insultingly late in the day he found himself accepted for membership of the Royal Yacht Squadron. The notion of rejecting the offered membership must have crossed his mind but that was not Lipton's style. He was now, as a member, eligible to enter for the Coveted King's Cup and at his only attempt his yacht won it by a mile.

He was anything but a mean-minded man but he must have derived great pleasure and deep satisfaction from the win. He did not, however, attend the dinner which customarily marked the end of Cowes Week, perhaps he had been kept waiting just too long. There was another intriguing point. Any further challenge for the America's cup would now come from the Royal Yacht Squadron, since he was now a member. Hitherto he had challenged in the colours of the Royal Ulster Yacht Club. How ironic it would be if at last he gained success in the America's Cup under the aegis of the very organisation which had held him at arms length for so long.

That was not going to happen and not for any animus he bore the Royal Yacht Squadron; there was no longer time for such considerations. Lipton had never lost the power of acute observation and despite the rejoicings on his behalf the previous summer he had recognised that the United States was not the glad, confident country he had known and so much loved. The Wall Street crash had transformed the "Roaring Twenties" into "Buddy Can you Spare a Dime".

No more boating, with the Uncle of Europe, Edward VII, or anyone else. An America's Cup contest could not but seem frivolous and unfeeling at a time of an economic crisis of catastrophic importance. When the country had abandoned the gold standard the games of millionaires would have provoked at best scornful indifference and at worst naked hostility.

In his biography Alex Waugh makes a very valid and well-taken point. It is that most great achievers wish to change society and it is the energy they bring to that task which enables them to succeed in their aims. No man ever had more energy than Lipton yet he was not a mover or shaker in any social or political sense. Very occasionally as in his aid to striking miners and share allocation to Michael Davitt of the Irish Nationalist Party there seems a hint of radical leanings but simple philanthropy is just as possible an answer.

He showed no interest whatsoever in, for example, the co-operative principles of Robert Owen and one could never have envisaged him being attracted to the later partnership principles of John Lewis. He had essentially built his business on the Crown Street shop principle - establish, consolidate, move on; establish, consolidate, move on.

Now, in the increasingly quiet house at Osidge, he could cast up his balance-sheet. He had never been ashamed of what he did for a living; the Kaiser's jibe had been a matter of pride to him. He had always been given to the homely aphorism and this never appears to better advantage than in his thoughts on salesmanship, contained in an address to a conference and which perhaps owed almost as much to John Westwood as to himself. We can leave him on this note, with his world fast closing in on him.

"In exactly the same way that the sailsman afloat should keep his craft trim and neat, his brasses burnished bright and his sails spotlessly clean, so should the salesman ashore be spruce and smart in his personal appearance - preserving at all times his own self-respect and the credit of his house and justifying to the full his claim to the title and position of 'an Ambassador of Commerce'.

The grand old man of yachting keeps an eye on preparations aboard Shamrock V.

Sir Thomas Lipton died on October 2nd 1931 at 7.15 p.m. Four doctors were in attendance and a few old acquaintances, but to his knowledge he had not a living relative.

THE WORLD'S LOSS

SIR THOMAS LIPTON

WORLD MOURNS PASSING OF SIR THOMAS LIPTON

PEER AND COMMONER

World's Best Sport Spent His Life Trying To Win the "Blooming Old Mug."

By VIRGIL PINKLEY
(U. P. Staff Correspondent)

LONDON, Oct. 3.—(U. P.)—Peer and commoner today mourned the death of Sir Thomas Lipton, veteran British sportsman who climbed from depressing poverty to wealth and international esteem, attempting to win "that blooming old mug."

Sir Thomas died at the age of 81 when his stout heart finally weakened. Without the advantages of education and financial backing, "Tommy" Lipton, as he liked to be called, started his business career as a messenger boy at the age of 11 and the salary of about 30 cents a week.

On rare holidays Tommy Lipton sailed small boats on the Clyde. His often futile efforts attracted his interest to ships that brought him eventual recognition as the greatest living yachtsman.

In 1869, Tommy Lipton with his meagre savings travelled to America as a steerage passenger and got his first glimpse of the country where he arrived years later aboard his luxurious steam yacht "Erin" to prepare for the arrival of his "Shamrock V." to compete for the America's cup.

Sir Thomas called the cup "that bloomin' old mug," and was not discouraged by his unsuccessful attempts to win it. He had plans for the construction of a "Shamrock CI" when he died.

Young Lipton worked as a grocery clerk and as a street car motorman in New Orleans when he came to the United States. He worked on plantations in South Carolina until he had saved about $500 and then went back to Scotland to start a grocery shop in which hung a huge sign, "Work Is Fun."

He formed certain business policies early in life and never deviated from them. He resolved never to take a partner, always to decline loans, and never to sign a bill.

Speaking of service and courtesy he once wrote: "The 20 shillings in a ship worker's pocket are just as good in my till as the pound in the landlord's pigskin purse. The workingman's wife with the basket on her arm is entitled to as much respect as the lady who comes to the store in her plush lined motorcar."

SIR THOMAS LIPTON'S WILL

Big Bequests for Glasgow

£80,000 FOR THE POOR

HOSPITALS AND INSTITUTIONS TO BENEFIT

The estate of Sir Thomas Lipton, whose funeral took place in Glasgow yesterday, is expected by his executors to exceed £1,000,000 gross.

In his will Sir Thomas leaves £80,000 to be applied in the City of Glasgow by his trustees for the benefit of poor mothers, of the working classes and their children.

After making certain specific bequests and legacies, including several to Glasgow infirmaries, Sir Thomas directs that the residue of his estate, which, it is anticipated, will amount to a very substantial sum, shall be divided among hospitals and institutions in the City of Glasgow and town of Cambuslang, and in the counties of London and Middlesex, including Southgate, where he died.

The house, policies, and estate at Osidge are to be preserved as a hostel for nurses in memory of Sir Thomas's mother.

£1,000,000 ESTATE

The official summary of the will, issued in Glasgow last night after a meeting of the executors, is in the following terms:—

Sir Thomas's will and two relative codicils are dated October 10, 1927. Another codicil is dated August 8, 1930.

Lord Inverforth; Mr Henry Ambrose Snelling, a director of Lipton, Ltd.; Colonel Duncan Neil, D.S.O., Greenock; Colonel Hugh B. Spens, D.S.O., Maclay Murray and Spens, solicitors, Glasgow; and James Brooks, late of Lipton, Ltd., are appointed as trustees.

Under a codicil dealing with his American property, Williard U. Taylor, attorney, 65 Wall Street, New York, and Sheldon Clark, vice-president of the Sinclair Oil Company, Chicago, are appointed trustees as regards the American properties, to act in accordance with the instructions of the British trustees.

There are a number of specific legacies to personal friends, employees past and present, and servants.

NURSES' HOME MEMORIAL.

As regards his estate at Osidge, Sir Thomas's trustees are directed to make over the house, policies and estate to such institution or persons or body corporate as they think fit, in order that it may be preserved as a hostel for nurses in memory of Sir Thomas's mother.

The trustees have also power to give such articles of furniture, etc., at Osidge to the hostel as they think fit, and a sum of £20,000 is left as an endowment for the hostel.

Under his will a sum of £100,000, less such sums as he may have given for this purpose during his lifetime, is left to be applied in the city of Glasgow by his trustees as they may think fit for the benefit of poor mothers of the working classes and their children. Sir Thomas during his lifetime gave £20,000 for this purpose, and accordingly the sum falling to be applied in this way will be £80,000.

DISPOSAL OF TROPHIES.

The gold Loving Cup presented to Sir Thomas by the people of the United States of America in 1900 is left to the New York Yacht Club. In making this bequest, the following words appear in Sir Thomas's will:—"I would like to add a personal note that they are the very best of sportsmen, and I appreciate very much the many kindnesses shown to me by them."

As regards Sir Thomas's collection of yacht racing cups and trophies, the trustees are given powers to hand over the collection in its entirety to some suitable museum or institution.

LEGACIES TO HOSPITALS.

The following specific legacies to charities are left by Sir Thomas:—

To the Royal Infirmary, Glasgow	£1000
To the Western Infirmary, Glasgow	£1000
To the Victoria Infirmary, Glasgow	£1000
To the Incorporated Glasgow Old Man's Friend Society and Old Woman's Home, 81 Rottenrow, Glasgow	£1000
To the Lipton Memorial Nurses' Home, Cambuslang	£3000
To the Grovelands Hospital, near London	£1000

THE RESIDUE.

In leaving these specific legacies, Sir Thomas provides that they are not to fetter or affect the discretion of his trustees in disposing of the residue of his estate in accordance with his will, or as to giving them named charities further sums in any way.

The residue of his estate is to be divided among hospitals and institutions in the city of Glasgow and town of Cambuslang and in the counties of London and Middlesex (including Southgate).

It is impossible to give any accurate estimate of Sir Thomas's estate, but it is anticipated that it will certainly exceed £1,000,000 gross.

cleared. The cortege had to pass through a long lane between spectators as it left the church to go to the cemetery.

PRINCIPAL MOURNERS.

The service in the church was conducted by the minister of St George's, the Rev. Dr D. A. Cameron Reid, and he was assisted by the Rev. Dr Lauchlan MacLean Watt, minister of the Cathedral.

Among the principal mourners were:—Lord Inverforth, the Marquis of Ailsa, Colonel D. F. D. Neil (who was a close personal friend, and represented Sir Thomas on board all the five Shamrocks in the races for the America's Cup; Colonel Hugh B. Spens and Mr T. P. Spens, Sir Thomas's firm of law agents, Messrs Maclay, Murray and Spens, Glasgow; Dr Fairweather, London; Sir Daniel M. Stevenson, Bt.; Sir David Mason, Sir Malcolm Campbell, Captain Hogarth, Mr William Davidson, chairman of R. and W. Davidson, Ltd.; Colonel Chalmers, Captain Colin Mitchell, Gourock; Mr Alex. Lauder and Miss Lauder (brother and niece of Sir Harry Lauder); and Mr J. Matheson Johnston, secretary of the Western Infirmary.

The Lord Provost of the city, Sir Thomas Kelly, attended in company with Magistrates, Councillors, and public officials, and places were reserved also for representatives of various organisations in which Sir Thomas Lipton took an interest.

The Royal Northern Yacht Club, of which Sir Thomas Lipton had been a member since 1899, was represented by Mr Fred J. Stephen, commodore, and Mr James Napier, rear-commodore; the Royal Clyde Yacht Club by Mr Ronald M. Teacher, Mr George Jackson, and Mr Francis A. Downes; and the Royal Ulster Yacht Club by Captain R. L. Henderson and Captain D. L. Ross. Numerous representatives of the branches of Liptons, Ltd., all over the country also attended.

"AN INSPIRING EXAMPLE."

The public composition of the congregation was illustrative of the general esteem which was inspired by the distinguished native of the city throughout the whole community.

The service was entirely devotional, including readings from the Old and New Testaments, with the singing of familiar Psalms and hymns. A very impressive feature of the service was an organ rendering of the lament, "The Flowers of the Forest."

In the course of prayer Dr MacLean Watt alluded to the inspiration of example which Sir Thomas Lipton had given to his fellows in the spirit of indomitableness by which he had conquered the adverse circumstances of his birth, the unresting and unwearying diligence of his industrious years, and the strength of soul that upheld him for the victory over the vicissitudes of his great adventure. He had remained humane in sympathy, tender in charity, generous in thought and deed; his thought of others was his richest example, and the blessing of his charity was his best reward.

THROUGH CROWDED STREETS.

It was appropriate that on its way from the church to the cemetery the cortege should pass along Crown Street, where Sir Thomas Lipton was born. Although rain was falling softly and persistently, this thoroughfare was deeply lined with people of the poorer classes, who waited patiently to pay their last tribute to one who had proved himself so well to be their friend and benefactor. A dense crowd assembled in Caledonia Road, and every window and vantage point in the vicinity of the Necropolis was fully occupied. The public were excluded from the cemetery, and only a comparatively few mourners witnessed the last rites. The interment took place in the family burial ground, situated in a secluded corner of the old cemetery, and marked by a granite monolith. The pall-bearers were Lord Inverforth, Colonel Neil, Lord Provost Sir Thomas Kelly, Mr John Westwood, Mr James Brooks, Mr H. A. Snelling, Colonel H. B. Spens, and Mr William Love. A brief committal service was conducted by the Rev. Dr Cameron Reid and the Rev. Dr MacLean Watt.

He had requested a simple service but stipulated that it must take place in Glasgow. He had loved his parents with an unfeigned devotion in life, he would be with them in death. He died a knight and baronet and of course the baronetcy went with him. The oft-talked of peerage had not materialised; ever a man who liked to tantalise and perhaps mislead reporters mischievously, he would sometimes talk as if the offer had been made and refused by him. Maybe so, it would surely have followed inevitably had he ever managed to regain the America's Cup.

News of his death was cabled to the United States and the lack of the element of surprise did not prevent a feeling of sorrow at the passing of one who had always been a well-wisher to the great Republic. His old friend and Presidential Candidate, Al Smith the Happy Warrior on receiving the news cabled by return "Your news fills me with great regret".

Mourners at Lipton's graveside at the Southern Necropolis, Glasgow.

Thousands of people line the streets of Glasgow as the cortege leaves the church.

No man who by his own efforts creates a vast fortune from scratch is likely to do it without the occasional descent into corner-cutting or sharp practice but to a really remarkable degree Lipton's standards were those of old-style probity. He could be ascetic without being censorious. He was himself a lifelong teetotaller and justified his abstention thus:

140

"Corkscrews have sunk more people than cork jackets will ever save" but he was a generous host and wine was the rule of the day at his small Osidge dinner parties.

He did not forget favours and old acquaintance. One of his first donations when he became successful was to the beat policeman who had been at Stobcross Street when he opened his shop there all those years ago. He was remarkably comfortable right across the complicated social strata of late Victorian society. It was said ironically that there was no one like Sir Thomas Lipton for putting the Kaiser at ease on his own Imperial yacht.

He had been faithful to his two guiding business principles, never take a partner and always decline a loan. There may have been an unspoken third, never take a wife, but if there was then it was never overtly formulated. His work for the furtherance of Anglo-American relations at a time when the two countries regarded each other with a prickly and irritable suspicion would of itself have been worth a peerage.

His will amounted to a sum in excess of one million pounds. He could have made flamboyant educational or political bequests but chose instead to relieve individual misery. He left £80,000 for the benefit of poor working-class mothers and their children (he had a shrewd and certain knowledge of which parent was more likely to be the salvation of such families) and he devoted a further £20,000 to the furtherance of the same object specifically in Glasgow.

He greatly cherished his American reputation as the world's most cheerful loser and he showed this by leaving the famous Loving Cup to the New York Yacht Club with the following comment:- "They are the very best of sportsmen and I appreciate very much the many kindnesses shown to me by them".

Now he was gone and much of his world was going with him. The headlines in the *Glasgow Herald* on the day of his funeral make interesting reading. As he, a great Scotsman, left the arena of human endeavour another, Ramsay MacDonald was being entrusted with the formation of a National Government which would try desperately to arrest the slump that marked the quickening of the irreversible decline of industrial Scotland. Even as the cortege fought its way through packed Glasgow streets there were violent demonstrations by the unemployed in another part of Lipton's own city.

In Europe things were even worse. The aged President of Germany, Hindenburg, was grimly trying to re-structure his Cabinet in a vain effort to slow the inexorable advance of totalitarianism. Alfonso XIII of Spain, long-known to Lipton, had just left his country in a destroyer bound for a life-time in

A TRIBUTE TO A GALLANT SOUL

exile. In Lipton's own last hours he may have remembered
having himself driven Alfonso and his new bride to take ship
on an earlier, brighter occasion.

There were two simultaneous funeral services. One took place
at the socially-smart Church of St. Columba's in Pont Street,
London. There foregathered some of his City acquaintances
and retired courtiers from time past. Lipton was an important

man in the City and it was right that his death should be duly marked.

His heart was in that other city where his funeral was even then taking place, in the church of St. George in the square of that name off Buchanan Street. Among the mourners were represented the Scottish nobility, and leading figures in commerce and industry. The Marquis of Ailsa attended and so too did Alex and Greta Lauder, brother and niece of the great Sir Harry.

Such was the press of people round the church and such the traffic congestion that the principal mourners were penned within the building for almost half-an-hour. Then, as a single piper played "The Flowers 0' the Forest" the coffin was brought out.

Slowly the hearse and the attendant cars threaded their way through the narrow city-centre streets, then out across the bridge to the south-side. The Gorbals and Hutchesontown streets were packed and silent. The cortege had by now reached the area where many of the old men, caps in hand to honour the slowly-passing dead, and old women would have known the younger Lipton personally, at least by sight.

Many years earlier, on receiving his knighthood, Thomas Johnstone Lipton had said that his greatest honour was the fact that he was a Glasgow man. He had honoured his native city with his life and at last he had come to the Southern Necropolis to lie with his parents and the brothers and sister so long dead. Now he too was dead, the great merchant was gone, the hopeful sailor come ashore.